The MCP Handbook

The MCP Handbook
A Practical Approach to AI Integration

Akash Kumar Nayak

Disclaimer
This book is informational. The publisher and author
disclaim all warranties and shall not be liable for any
damages arising from its use. Consult professionals for
specific advice.

Trademarks
All trademarks are the property of their respective owners.

Publisher
Akash Kumar Nayak
ISBN 9798316945474

INTRODUCTION

Artificial intelligence, particularly the advent of powerful Large Language Models (LLMs), is revolutionizing how we interact with technology. We're moving beyond simple commands towards dynamic conversations, complex problem-solving, and AI-driven automation. Yet, a significant hurdle remains: how do we seamlessly and securely integrate these intelligent models into the vast landscape of existing software applications, tools, and data sources?

For AI to reach its full potential, it can't remain isolated. It needs to interact with the digital world – to access real-time information, trigger actions in other applications, and leverage specialized tools. Historically, connecting AI models to external systems has often involved bespoke, brittle, and complex integrations, creating significant development overhead and security challenges. Each new connection required reinventing the wheel, hindering scalability and interoperability.

Enter the **Model Context Protocol (MCP)**. MCP emerges as a standardized solution to this critical integration challenge. It provides a common language, a set of rules and structures that allow AI models and external applications or tools (which we'll call "servers" in the MCP world) to communicate effectively, securely, and predictably. Think of it as a universal adapter or a diplomatic protocol enabling fruitful conversations between the world of AI reasoning and the world of software functionality.

This book is your comprehensive guide to understanding and implementing the Model Context Protocol. Whether you're a developer building AI-powered features, an architect designing integrated systems, or a technical professional seeking to harness the power of connected AI, this practical, actionable resource will equip you with the necessary knowledge and skills.

Inside, you will discover:
- **The Foundations:** What MCP is, why it's needed, and its core components – Tools, Resources, and Prompts.
- **Implementation Deep Dive:** Step-by-step guides to building both MCP Servers (exposing capabilities) and Clients (connecting AI applications).
- **Mastering Interactions:** Detailed exploration of designing effective Tools, leveraging Resources for context, and using Prompts for optimization.
- **Security by Design:** Essential best practices for securing your MCP integrations, covering authentication, authorization, data handling, and more.
- **Advanced Concepts:** Exploring sophisticated features like notifications, hierarchical systems, interactive workflows, and streaming results.
- **The Ecosystem & Future:** Understanding the community, real-world applications, and the exciting future roadmap for MCP.

Written in a clear, accessible style with practical examples and helpful analogies, this book aims to demystify MCP and empower you to build the next generation of intelligent, integrated applications.

We'll cut through the jargon and focus on what you need to know to get started and succeed.

The era of siloed AI is ending. The future lies in collaboration between AI models and the rich ecosystem of software tools and services we rely on daily. MCP provides the crucial bridge to that future. Let's embark on this journey together and unlock the transformative potential of truly integrated artificial intelligence.

Table of Contents

11

CHAPTER 1

Introduction to the Model Context Protocol: The USB-C of AI

Welcome! You're standing at the edge of a revolution – the artificial intelligence revolution. AI models are transforming industries, automating tasks, and unlocking insights we never thought possible. From generating creative text to analyzing complex datasets, AI is rapidly becoming an essential tool in the developer's arsenal.

But let's be honest. Integrating these powerful AI models into our applications, tools, and workflows can feel like navigating a chaotic mess of incompatible plugs and tangled wires. Every AI model seems to speak its own dialect, requiring custom-built connectors and painstaking integration efforts for every single application you want to power. It's inefficient, costly, and slows down innovation precisely when we need to accelerate.

Imagine a world before USB-C. Remember the drawer full of different chargers? One for your phone, another for your camera, a different one for your laptop, maybe even a proprietary connector for that old MP3 player. Each new device meant potentially needing a new, specific adapter. It was cumbersome, wasteful, and frustrating.

That's essentially the state of AI integration today. But what if there was a universal standard? A single, elegant solution that allows any AI model to seamlessly connect and communicate with any application?

Enter the Model Context Protocol (MCP). Think of it, quite simply, as the USB-C of AI.

What is MCP and Why is it a Game-Changer?

The Model Context Protocol (MCP) is an emerging open standard designed to streamline the way applications interact with AI models. At its core, MCP defines a **standardized format and procedure** for packaging and exchanging the necessary information – the "context" – that an AI model needs to perform a task, and for receiving the results back.

Just like USB-C standardized the physical connector *and* the communication protocols (power delivery, data transfer, video output) between devices, MCP standardizes how we "plug" AI models into our software systems and how they "talk" to each other.

Why is this so crucial? In the rapidly evolving AI landscape, new models with diverse capabilities are appearing constantly. Simultaneously, developers want to embed AI intelligence into an ever-growing number of applications, from simple chatbots to complex enterprise systems. Without a standard, this leads directly to a crippling problem.

The "M×N Problem": Untangling the AI Integration Spaghetti

Let's visualize the current challenge. Imagine you have **M** different AI models you want to use (e.g., a language model for text generation, an image recognition model, a sentiment analysis model). Now, imagine you have **N** different applications or tools where you want to integrate these models (e.g., your CRM, a customer support platform, a data analytics dashboard, a content management system).

Without a standard like MCP, each specific model needs a custom integration for *each* specific application. This creates an **M × N integration problem**.

- Want to use 3 models in 4 applications? That's 3 * 4 = **12** unique integrations to build, test, and maintain.
- Want to add just one more model? That's another 4 integrations.

- Want to add one more application? That's another 3 integrations.

The complexity explodes exponentially. It's like needing 12 different, custom-made adapter cables just to connect your 3 devices to your 4 power outlets. This "integration spaghetti" is:

- **Time-consuming:** Developers spend valuable time writing boilerplate code instead of building features.
- **Expensive:** More development hours mean higher costs.
- **Brittle:** Custom integrations are prone to breaking when either the model or the application updates.
- **Stifling:** The sheer effort discourages experimentation and the adoption of new AI capabilities.

MCP offers a beautifully simple alternative: the "M+N" solution.

With MCP, you don't build M×N custom bridges. Instead:

1. Each of your **M** models implements the **MCP standard interface** (like having a USB-C port).
2. Each of your **N** applications implements the **MCP standard interface** (like also having a USB-C port).

Now, connecting any model to any application becomes trivial. They both speak the same language! You only need to implement the standard M times (once for each model) and N times (once for each application), resulting in **M + N implementations** of the *same* standard.

- Using our example: 3 models + 4 applications = **7** implementations of the MCP standard.

Suddenly, the integration landscape looks much cleaner, much more manageable, and infinitely more scalable. Just like plugging any USB-C device into any USB-C port – it just works.

Key Benefits of Adopting MCP: The Universal Advantage

The shift from M×N chaos to M+N simplicity brings tangible benefits:

1. **Standardization:** This is the core value proposition, the USB-C effect. MCP provides a common language and structure for AI interactions. This means predictable integrations, reduced developer guesswork, and easier collaboration. Teams can build reusable components knowing they'll interface correctly.
2. **Efficiency:** Drastically reduces the time and effort needed to integrate AI. Instead of bespoke code for every connection, you implement a single standard. This accelerates development cycles, lowers costs, and frees up developers to focus on innovation rather than plumbing. Think of the time saved by not searching for that specific charger!
3. **Security:** Standardizing the communication protocol allows for standardized security practices. Defining context boundaries and interaction patterns clearly makes it easier to implement robust security measures, conduct audits, and manage access control consistently across all integrations, rather than securing dozens of unique, custom endpoints. USB-C also has defined protocols for secure power delivery and data handling, reducing risks.
4. **Scalability & Flexibility:** Adding new AI models or connecting existing models to new applications becomes incredibly easy. Want to try out a cutting-edge new model? As long as it supports MCP (or you create an MCP adapter for it), plugging it into your ecosystem is straightforward. Need to embed AI into another internal tool? If the tool speaks MCP, connection is simple. This future-proofs your architecture and encourages experimentation. Your system grows elegantly, not exponentially complex.

MCP vs. Traditional API Integrations: A Comparative Overview

You might be thinking, "Don't we already have APIs for this?" Yes, but traditional API integrations typically contribute to the M×N problem. Here's a high-level comparison:

Feature	Traditional API Integrations	Model Context Protocol (MCP)	USB-C Analogy
Approach	Often bespoke, point-to-point	Standardized, protocol-based	Proprietary Connectors vs. Universal USB-C Port
Complexity	High (M×N integrations)	Low (M+N implementations of the standard)	Needing M*N adapters vs. M+N devices/ports
Flexibility	Lower; adding models/apps requires new integrations	High; easily swap or add compliant components	Hard to swap devices vs. Easy plug-and-play
Maintenance	High; maintain many unique integrations	Lower; maintain standard implementations	Maintaining many chargers vs. one standard

Efficiency	Lower; significant integration effort per link	Higher; reduced boilerplate, faster integration	Time wasted finding chargers vs. quick connection
Interoperabil ity	Often limited, vendor-specific	High; designed for cross-vendor compatibility	Devices work across brands
Security	Varied, depends on each bespoke implementati on	Standardized approach enables consistent security	Defined safety standards vs. variable quality

While specific APIs will always exist, MCP doesn't necessarily replace them entirely. Instead, it provides a standardized *layer* for the crucial task of exchanging context and results with AI models, simplifying what is often the most complex and rapidly changing part of the integration puzzle.

The Road Ahead

The Model Context Protocol represents a fundamental shift towards a more open, efficient, and scalable AI ecosystem. It promises to break down silos, accelerate innovation, and make the power of diverse AI models accessible to a much wider range of applications and developers. It's the universal adapter we desperately need in this era of intelligent machines.

In this book, we'll dive deep into the mechanics of MCP. We'll explore its architecture, show you how to implement it in your projects, and guide you through practical examples. Get ready to leave the tangled mess of custom integrations behind and embrace the clean, standardized power of the Model Context Protocol – the USB-C of AI. Let's begin!

CHAPTER 2

Core Concepts and Architecture: Hosts, Clients, and Servers

In Chapter 1, we introduced the Model Context Protocol (MCP) as the "USB-C of AI," a much-needed standard to simplify how applications and AI models connect and communicate. We saw how it promises to replace the tangled M×N mess of custom integrations with a clean, scalable M+N approach.

Now, it's time to look under the hood. How does MCP actually achieve this? What are the fundamental building blocks that make this standardized communication possible?

At its heart, MCP utilizes a familiar pattern in software architecture: the **client-server model**. But it adapts this model specifically for the unique needs of AI integration. Understanding this structure is key to effectively using and implementing MCP. Let's meet the three core players in the MCP architecture: **Hosts**, **Clients**, and **Servers**.

The Client-Server Foundation of MCP

Before diving into the specific MCP roles, let's quickly refresh the basic client-server concept. Think about browsing the web:

- Your **web browser** (like Chrome or Firefox) acts as the **client**. It *requests* information (a webpage).
- The **web server** hosting the website acts as the **server**. It *listens* for requests, processes them, and *serves* back the requested information (the webpage data).

MCP leverages this fundamental request-response pattern. An application needs something done by an AI, so it makes a request. A service provides that AI capability and sends back a response. However, MCP introduces specific roles to manage this interaction within the AI context.

Understanding MCP Hosts: The AI Applications We Interact With

What it is: The **MCP Host** is the application or tool that a user directly interacts with and which *needs* to leverage AI capabilities to perform its functions. Think of it as the main stage where the action happens.

Its Role:

- Provides the user interface or the primary workflow.
- Determines *when* and *why* an AI capability is needed.
- Orchestrates the overall task, potentially involving multiple AI interactions.
- Initiates requests for AI processing via one or more MCP Clients.
- Receives results back from MCP Clients and presents them to the user or uses them in its workflow.

Analogy: If MCP is the USB-C standard, the **Host is like your laptop or smartphone**. It's the primary device you use, the one running the applications (like a word processor, photo editor, or coding environment) that might need to connect to external capabilities (like a printer, external storage, or, in our case, an AI model).

Examples of MCP Hosts:

- An Integrated Development Environment (IDE) like VS Code using an AI model for code completion.
- A customer support chatbot interface that needs an AI to understand user queries and generate responses.
- A data analysis platform using an AI model to identify trends or anomalies.
- A graphic design tool leveraging an AI model for image generation or enhancement.

The Host is the *consumer* of AI capabilities within the MCP framework.

The Role of MCP Clients: Managing Connections and Communication

What it is: The **MCP Client** acts as the dedicated intermediary or *connector manager* between the Host application and *one specific* MCP Server. It lives within or is tightly coupled with the Host application.

Its Role:

- Establishes and manages the connection to a single MCP Server.
- Receives requests from the Host application.
- **Crucially, it packages the necessary context (data, instructions, history) into the standardized MCP format.**
- Sends the standardized request to its paired MCP Server.
- Receives the standardized response from the Server.
- **Unpacks the response** and delivers the results back to the Host application in a way the Host understands.
- Handles the specifics of the MCP protocol communication (think error handling, message sequencing, etc.).

Analogy: Continuing the USB-C analogy, the **Client is like a specific USB-C *port* on your laptop**. Each port is dedicated to managing the connection and communication protocol for *one* device plugged into it at a time. It knows how to "speak USB-C" (or, here, MCP) to negotiate power, data transfer, etc., with the connected device (the Server).

Key Point: A single Host application might utilize *multiple* MCP Clients, each connecting to a different MCP Server, to access various AI capabilities. For instance, an IDE (Host) might have one Client talking to a code-completion Server and another Client talking to a code-explanation Server.

Exploring MCP Servers: Exposing Capabilities and Connecting to Resources

What it is: The **MCP Server** is the component that actually *provides* or *exposes* a specific AI capability. It's the "engine" that does the AI work or connects to the underlying AI model or resource.

Its Role:

- Listens for incoming connections and requests from its paired MCP Client.
- Receives the standardized MCP request.
- **Understands the MCP format and extracts the context needed for the task.**
- Performs the requested AI processing. This might involve:
    - Directly running an AI model inference.
    - Calling an external AI model API (like OpenAI, Anthropic, a local model, etc.).
    - Accessing a database or other knowledge source needed by the model.
    - Executing specific tools or functions based on the request.
-
- **Packages the results (output, errors, metadata) into the standardized MCP format.**
- Sends the standardized response back to the MCP Client.

Analogy: The **Server is like the external device you plug into the USB-C port** – the printer, the external hard drive, the webcam. It's the specialized tool that *provides a specific function* (printing, storage, video capture) and understands how to communicate its capabilities and results via the USB-C standard (MCP).

Examples of MCP Servers:

- A wrapper around a specific Large Language Model (LLM) exposing text generation capabilities via MCP.
- A service connected to an image recognition model that accepts image data via MCP and returns object labels.
- An adapter for a company's internal knowledge base, allowing an AI model (accessed via the Server) to query it through an MCP request.

The Crucial One-to-One Client-Server Relationship

It's vital to emphasize the relationship: **Each MCP Client connects to exactly one MCP Server.** This one-to-one pairing is fundamental to how MCP simplifies things.

- **Host-to-Many:** A Host application can instantiate and manage *multiple* MCP Clients simultaneously.
- **Client-to-One:** Each of those MCP Clients is dedicated to managing the communication protocol and connection state for *only one* specific MCP Server.

Think back to the laptop (Host). It has multiple USB-C ports (Clients). You plug one printer cable (Server connection) into one port, one external drive cable (another Server connection) into another port. Each port (Client) manages its dedicated connection.

This design provides:

1. **Clear Separation:** The Host worries about the application logic, the Client worries about MCP communication for *one* connection, and the Server worries about providing the *specific* AI capability.
2. **Modularity:** You can easily add new AI capabilities to your Host by simply adding a new Client-Server pair, without disrupting existing integrations.

3. **Targeted Communication:** The Host knows exactly which Client to talk to for a specific AI task, and that Client knows exactly which Server provides it.

(Conceptual Diagram Description):

Imagine a central box labeled "**MCP Host** (e.g., IDE)". Emanating from this Host box are two smaller boxes *inside* or *attached* to it, labeled "**MCP Client A** (Code Completion Port)" and "**MCP Client B** (Debugging Helper Port)".

- MCP Client A has a single line connecting it outwards to a separate box labeled "**MCP Server A** (Code Completion LLM Service)".
- MCP Client B has a single line connecting it outwards to a different separate box labeled "**MCP Server B** (Code Analysis & Debug Tool)".

This visually represents the Host using multiple Clients, each dedicated to a single Server.

Putting It All Together

So, the typical flow looks like this:

1. User interacts with the **Host** application (e.g., types code in an IDE).
2. The **Host** decides it needs AI assistance (e.g., code completion).
3. The **Host** tells the appropriate **MCP Client** (the one connected to the code completion service) what it needs.
4. The **MCP Client** packages the current code, cursor position, and other relevant info into a standard MCP request.
5. The **MCP Client** sends this request to its paired **MCP Server**.

6. The **MCP Server** receives the request, unpacks it, potentially calls an LLM, gets the completion suggestion.
7. The **MCP Server** packages the suggestion into a standard MCP response.
8. The **MCP Server** sends the response back to the **MCP Client**.
9. The **MCP Client** receives the response, unpacks it, and gives the suggestion back to the **Host**.
10. The **Host** displays the code completion suggestion to the user.

Conclusion

Understanding the roles of the Host, Client, and Server is fundamental to grasping the MCP architecture.

- **Host:** The user-facing application that needs AI.
- **Client:** The protocol-aware connector manager within the Host, dedicated to one Server.
- **Server:** The provider of the specific AI capability, speaking MCP.

This clear separation of concerns, built on a client-server foundation and emphasizing the one-to-one Client-Server relationship, is what allows MCP to deliver on its promise of standardized, efficient, and scalable AI integration.

In the next chapter, we'll delve deeper into the actual *content* of that standardized communication – the context package itself and what information typically flows between the Client and Server.

CHAPTER 3

The Building Blocks: Tools, Resources, and Prompts

Welcome to the engine room of the Model Context Protocol! In the previous chapters, we explored the "why" behind MCP – the need for a standardized way for AI models and applications to communicate effectively. Now, we dive into the "how." This chapter introduces the three fundamental building blocks that make MCP work: **Tools**, **Resources**, and **Prompts**.

Think of building a sophisticated AI assistant. You need ways for the AI to *do* things (like book appointments), ways for it to *know* things (like your current schedule), and ways for *you* to guide its behavior for the best results. Tools, Resources, and Prompts provide exactly these capabilities within the MCP framework. Understanding these core components is crucial for harnessing the full potential of AI integration. Let's break them down.

Tools (Model-controlled): Empowering AI to Take Action

Imagine giving your AI assistant a set of specialized tools – a wrench to fix things, a phone to make calls, a pen to write messages. In MCP, **Tools** are precisely that: they are functions or capabilities that the *AI model* can choose to use to perform actions or interact with the outside world.

- **Definition:** Tools represent actions or operations the AI model can invoke. They are essentially functions exposed to the model, allowing it to go beyond generating text and actively *do* things in the digital or even physical world (via connected systems).

- **Control:** Tools are **model-controlled**. This means the AI decides *when* and *how* to use a specific tool based on the user's request and the context. The application defines *what* tools are available, but the model selects and executes them.
- **Analogy:** Think of a skilled chef (the AI model) in a well-equipped kitchen (the application environment). The knives, ovens, and mixers are the **Tools**. The chef decides which tool to use (e.g., "I need the whisk tool to beat these eggs") based on the recipe (the user's request).
- **Examples:**
  - **API Calls:** Sending data to an external service (e.g., using a book_flight tool that calls an airline's API).
  - **Database Operations:** Executing commands to update information (e.g., a create_calendar_event tool that adds an entry to a database).
  - **Sending Notifications:** Triggering alerts or messages (e.g., an send_email tool).
  - **Executing Code:** Running specific scripts or functions within the application's environment.

Tools are the action-oriented part of MCP, enabling AI to become an active participant rather than just a passive respondent.

Resources (Application-controlled): Providing Essential Context to AI

If Tools are what the AI can *do*, **Resources** are what the AI can *know*. For an AI to act intelligently, it needs access to relevant, up-to-date information. Resources provide this context.

- **Definition:** Resources represent specific pieces of data or information that the application makes available to the AI model. They act as controlled access points to the application's state or external data sources.
- **Control:** Resources are **application-controlled**. The application determines *what* information is available as a Resource and ensures the data provided is accurate and current. The AI model can request access to a Resource, but the application manages the data itself.
- **Analogy:** Continuing the chef analogy, **Resources** are the ingredients in the pantry and refrigerator (the application's data stores). The chef (AI model) knows they can request "tomatoes" (access the user_profile Resource), but the kitchen manager (the application) ensures the tomatoes are fresh and provides them when requested.
- **Examples:**
  - **User Profile Data:** Accessing information like name, email, preferences (user_profile Resource).
  - **Product Catalog:** Fetching details about available products (product_database Resource).
  - **Current Weather:** Getting real-time weather information (weather_api_data Resource).
  - **Document Content:** Accessing the text of a specific file (document_text Resource).
  - **GET Endpoints:** As you noted, Resources often function similarly to HTTP GET

endpoints in web development – they provide a way to retrieve a specific piece of information without changing the underlying system state.

Resources ensure the AI model operates with the necessary background information, leading to more relevant and accurate responses and actions.

Prompts (User-controlled): Optimizing AI Interactions

While Tools let the AI act and Resources let it know, **Prompts** allow the *user* (or developer) to guide *how* the AI approaches a task. They are templates or instructions that shape the AI's behavior for specific use cases.

- **Definition:** Prompts are pre-defined structures or templates for interacting with the AI model, designed to elicit optimal responses for recurring tasks or specific contexts. They often include placeholders for dynamic information.
- **Control:** Prompts are typically **user-controlled** or **developer-controlled**. Users or developers craft these prompts to streamline interactions and ensure the AI receives instructions in the most effective format.
- **Analogy:** Think of Prompts as standardized order forms at a restaurant. Instead of vaguely telling the chef "make me food," you use a form (order_pizza Prompt) that specifies "Size: [Large], Toppings: [Pepperoni, Mushrooms], Crust: [Thin]." This ensures the chef gets the exact information needed in the right format.
- **Examples:**

- Summarization Prompt: "Summarize the following document: [Document Content]. Focus on the key findings and action items."
- Email Generation Prompt: "Draft a polite follow-up email to [Recipient Name] regarding our meeting about [Topic]. Mention that the meeting notes are attached."
- Code Generation Prompt: "Write a Python function named [FunctionName] that takes [InputParameters] and returns [ExpectedOutput]. Include error handling for [SpecificErrorCondition]."

Prompts act as blueprints for interaction, making communication with the AI more efficient, predictable, and tailored to specific needs.

How They Work Together: A Symphony of Interaction

The true power of MCP emerges when Tools, Resources, and Prompts work in concert. Let's illustrate with a simple scenario:

Scenario: A user asks their AI assistant, "What's on my schedule for tomorrow, and can you book a 30-minute meeting with Alex about the project launch?"

1. **User Request:** The initial request comes in.
2. **Prompt (Optional):** The application might use a pre-defined schedule_and_book Prompt to structure the interaction, ensuring the AI understands the dual nature of the request.

3. **Resource Access:** The AI model identifies the need for schedule information. It requests access to the user_calendar **Resource**. The application provides the relevant calendar data for tomorrow.
4. **Information Processing:** The AI processes the calendar data retrieved via the Resource.
5. **Tool Invocation:** The AI determines it needs to book a meeting. It identifies the book_meeting **Tool** as the appropriate action.
6. **Tool Execution:** The AI invokes the book_meeting Tool, potentially passing parameters like attendee ("Alex"), duration ("30 minutes"), and topic ("Project Launch"). The application's code behind the book_meeting Tool interacts with the calendar system API to create the event.
7. **Response Generation:** The AI formulates a response to the user, combining the information from the user_calendar Resource and the outcome of the book_meeting Tool (e.g., "Tomorrow you have a meeting at 10 AM. I have successfully booked a 30-minute meeting with Alex about the project launch at 2 PM.").

In this flow, the Resource provided context (schedule), the Tool performed an action (booking), and a Prompt could have been used to structure the initial request for clarity. This interplay allows for complex, multi-step tasks to be handled seamlessly.

By understanding Tools, Resources, and Prompts, you grasp the core mechanics of the Model Context Protocol. These components provide a flexible yet standardized framework for building sophisticated applications where AI models can access information, take meaningful actions, and be guided for optimal performance. In the next chapter, we'll delve deeper into the practical implementation details and explore how to define and use these building blocks in your own projects.

CHAPTER 4

Communication Channels: Understanding MCP Transports

In Chapter 3, we unpacked the core building blocks of the Model Context Protocol: Tools, Resources, and Prompts. Now, let's look at the plumbing – how do the different components, the AI model (Server) and the application (Client), actually exchange messages containing these blocks? This is where MCP **Transports** come in.

Think of transports as the delivery methods for MCP messages. Just like you can send a package via local courier or international air mail depending on the distance and need, MCP offers different transport mechanisms suited for various integration scenarios. Choosing the right transport ensures efficient and reliable communication between your application and the AI model.

This chapter will guide you through the primary communication channels currently used in MCP and give you a glimpse into the future. We'll cover:

1. **Local Integrations:** Using standard input/output (stdio) for processes running on the same machine.
2. **Remote Communication:** Leveraging Server-Sent Events (SSE) over HTTP for network-based interactions.
3. **Future Directions:** The planned evolution towards Streamable HTTP.

Understanding these transports is key to setting up your MCP integration correctly, whether you're building a simple command-line tool or a complex, distributed web service.

Local Integrations with stdio (Standard Input/Output)

Imagine two programs running on your computer that need to talk directly to each other. The simplest, most fundamental way they can do this is through their standard communication channels: Standard Input (stdin), Standard Output (stdout), and Standard Error (stderr), collectively known as stdio.

- **What it is:** stdio refers to the pre-connected input and output streams that operating systems provide to every running process. A program reads from its stdin and writes to its stdout.
- **MCP Context:** In MCP, the stdio transport is used when the Client (your application) and the Server (the AI model process) are running **on the same machine**. The Client process starts the Server process and then communicates with it by writing MCP messages to the Server's stdin and reading messages from the Server's stdout.
- **Analogy:** Think of it like two people communicating via pneumatic tubes connecting their desks directly. One person writes a message (MCP request), puts it in the tube (writes to stdout), and it arrives directly at the other person's desk (stdin). The reply comes back through a return tube.
- **Use Cases:**
    - Command-line interface (CLI) tools that integrate AI capabilities.
    - Desktop applications embedding a local AI model.
    - Development environments where simplicity and direct process communication are prioritized.
- **Characteristics:**

- o **Direct:** No network overhead.
- o **Simple:** Relies on fundamental OS-level process communication.
- o **Local Only:** Cannot be used for communication across different machines.

The stdio transport is ideal for tightly integrated, same-machine scenarios where network communication is unnecessary or undesirable.

Remote Communication with SSE (Server-Sent Events) via HTTP

What happens when your application and the AI model live on different machines, potentially separated by a network or the internet? We need a web-friendly way to communicate. This is where Server-Sent Events (SSE) come into play.

- • **What it is:** SSE is a standard web technology that allows a server to push data updates to a client over a single, long-lived HTTP connection. Unlike the traditional request-response model of HTTP, SSE enables the server to *initiate* sending data to the client once an initial connection is established.
- • **MCP Context:** The SSE transport uses standard HTTP(S) for communication. The Client (your application) makes an initial HTTP request to the Server (the AI model endpoint). The Server keeps this connection open and sends MCP messages back to the Client as events occur (e.g., the model generates a response, requests a Tool use, etc.). Client messages are typically sent via separate HTTP POST requests to a designated endpoint on the Server.

- **Analogy:** Think of subscribing to a live news feed ticker (like those on financial news channels). You establish the connection once (tune into the channel), and then the server (news station) continuously sends updates (news headlines) as they happen, without you having to ask each time.
- **Use Cases:**
  - Web applications interacting with a remote AI model service.
  - Distributed systems where the application frontend and AI backend are separate services.
  - Scenarios requiring real-time updates from the AI model (e.g., streaming responses).
- **Characteristics:**
  - **Network-Based:** Uses standard HTTP/HTTPS, suitable for web and distributed systems.
  - **Server-to-Client Streaming:** Efficient for the AI model (Server) to send multiple messages or stream responses to the application (Client).
  - **Standardized:** Built on well-established web technologies.
  - **Primarily Unidirectional (Server Push):** While the client *can* send messages (via separate POSTs), the core SSE mechanism is about the server pushing data.

SSE provides a robust and standardized way to handle communication between networked MCP Clients and Servers, particularly well-suited for scenarios where the AI model needs to send multiple messages or stream its output.

Looking Ahead: The Transition to Streamable HTTP

Technology evolves, and so does MCP. While stdio and SSE serve current needs well, the community is looking towards **Streamable HTTP** as a potential future transport mechanism.

- **What it is (Conceptually):** Streamable HTTP refers to newer HTTP capabilities (like enhancements in HTTP/2 and HTTP/3, or technologies like WebTransport) that allow for more efficient, potentially bidirectional streaming over a single connection. Unlike SSE (primarily server-to-client push) or traditional request-response, these newer approaches aim to make full-duplex (two-way) communication over HTTP more natural and performant.
- **Potential Benefits for MCP:**
  - **Efficiency:** Potentially reduces overhead compared to managing separate connections or frequent polling.
  - **Bidirectional Streaming:** Could simplify the interaction model by allowing both Client and Server to stream messages freely over the same connection, potentially improving responsiveness for complex interactions involving multiple Tool calls and Resource requests.
  - **Modern Standard:** Aligns with the evolution of web protocols.
- **Status:** This is currently an area of exploration and future planning within the MCP ecosystem. The goal is to leverage advancements in web standards to make communication even more seamless and efficient.

Keep an eye on MCP developments, as Streamable HTTP promises to refine remote communication further, offering a potentially more integrated and efficient alternative to the current SSE-based approach for networked scenarios.

Choosing the right transport – stdio for local simplicity or SSE (and potentially Streamable HTTP in the future) for networked flexibility – is a foundational step in building your MCP-powered application. With the building blocks from Chapter 3 and the communication channels covered here, you're now equipped to understand the core architecture of an MCP integration. In the following chapters, we'll start putting this knowledge into practice.

CHAPTER 5

Setting Up Your Development Environment for MCP

Alright, it's time to roll up our sleeves and prepare our workstations! In the previous chapters, we explored the "what" and "why" of the Model Context Protocol, delving into its core components (Tools, Resources, Prompts) and communication methods (Transports). Now, we transition to the "how" from a developer's perspective: setting up your environment to actually build applications using MCP. Taking the time to establish a solid foundation now will save significant effort down the line and make the development process much smoother.

Getting your development environment ready is the crucial first step before writing any code. It involves installing the necessary libraries (SDKs - Software Development Kits), knowing where to find the official rules of the road (the MCP specification), and discovering resources to help you along the way. Think of it as preparing your workshop before starting a new project – having the right tools and plans readily available makes all the difference.

This chapter is your practical guide to getting started. We'll cover:

1. **Installing Necessary SDKs and Tools:** Finding and setting up the right libraries for your preferred programming language.
2. **Understanding the MCP Specification and SDKs:** Locating and making sense of the core protocol definition and the specific library documentation you'll be using.

3. **Exploring Development Resources:** Discovering where to find help, examples, community support, and best practices.

Don't worry, setting up for MCP is designed to be straightforward, leveraging familiar package managers and development practices. Let's get you ready to build!

Gearing Up: Installing SDKs and Tools

The MCP community aims to provide Software Development Kits (SDKs) for popular programming languages to make integration easier. These SDKs are invaluable because they abstract away many of the lower-level details of the protocol. They typically handle the complexities of serializing and deserializing messages according to the spec, managing the chosen transport communication (stdio or SSE), and performing basic validation, letting you focus on the unique logic of your application and how it leverages AI capabilities.

While the specific packages and installation commands will vary depending on your language and project setup, here's a general guide for common languages. Remember to also check for any prerequisites, such as minimum required versions for your language runtime (e.g., Python 3.8+, Node.js 18+, specific JDK versions).

- **Python:** Look for the official MCP Python SDK, likely available via pip, Python's standard package installer. You'd typically install it within a dedicated virtual environment for your project to manage dependencies effectively:

```
# Example: Create and activate a virtual environment first
# python -m venv .venv
```

```
# source .venv/bin/activate  # On Linux/macOS
# .\.venv\Scripts\activate  # On Windows
```

pip install mcp-sdk-python # Hypothetical package name

*
- **TypeScript/JavaScript:** For Node.js
  environments or front-end frameworks, an SDK
  would likely be available on the npm registry.
  You'd add it as a project dependency using npm or
  yarn:

```
# Using npm
npm install @mcp/sdk-ts # Hypothetical package name

# Or using yarn
yarn add @mcp/sdk-ts # Hypothetical package name
```

*
- **Java:** For Java developers (which often includes
  Android or Kotlin developers targeting the JVM),
  the SDK would typically be distributed as a library
  via Maven Central or another artifact repository.
  You would declare the dependency in your
  project's build configuration file (pom.xml for
  Maven or build.gradle/build.gradle.kts for Gradle).

```
<dependency>
    <groupId>org.mcp-protocol</groupId>
    <artifactId>mcp-sdk-java</artifactId>
    <version>LATEST_VERSION</version> </dependency>
```kotlin
// Hypothetical Gradle Kotlin DSL Dependency in
build.gradle.kts
```
```

```
implementation("org.mcp-protocol:mcp-sdk-
java:LATEST_VERSION") // Replace with actual latest
version
```

-
- **C# / .NET:** Developers working within the .NET ecosystem would likely find the SDK distributed as a NuGet package. This can be easily installed using the .NET Command Line Interface (CLI) or through the NuGet Package Manager interface within Visual Studio.

```
# Using the .NET CLI
dotnet add package MCP.Sdk.Net # Hypothetical package name
```

-
- **Kotlin:** While Kotlin developers can readily use the Java SDK when targeting the JVM or Android (thanks to Kotlin's interoperability with Java), keep an eye out for potential dedicated Kotlin Multiplatform SDKs. These might emerge to offer more idiomatic Kotlin APIs or target additional platforms like Kotlin/Native or Kotlin/JS directly. Always check the official resources for the most current Kotlin-specific options.

Key Action: It cannot be stressed enough: **always refer to the official MCP documentation portal** for the definitive, up-to-date package names, installation instructions, version compatibility information, and any platform-specific prerequisites for your chosen language. Relying on outdated blog posts or examples can lead to compatibility issues or missing important features or security updates.

Understanding the Blueprints: The MCP Specification and SDK Documentation

While SDKs provide a convenient layer of abstraction, having a grasp of the underlying protocol specification is invaluable for troubleshooting, advanced customization, or even contributing back to the ecosystem.

- **The MCP Specification:** This document is the ultimate source of truth. It rigorously defines the protocol's rules, the exact structure and required fields for every message type (like ToolRequest, ToolResponse, ResourceRequest, ResourceResponse, etc.), the expected sequence of messages for different interactions, error handling guidelines, and the requirements for implementing the stdio and SSE transports.
    - **Where to Find It:** Look for a clearly marked link to the "Specification" or "Protocol Definition" on the main MCP website or developer portal. It might be hosted in a version control system like GitHub (allowing you to see revision history) or presented on a dedicated documentation site.
    - **How to Read It:** You likely don't need to memorize the entire spec on day one. Start by understanding the high-level architecture. Then, focus on the structure of the most common messages you'll be sending or receiving. Pay attention to the interaction flows relevant to your use case – for instance, the exact sequence of messages involved when an AI model decides to use a Tool provided by your application. Referring back to the spec can

clarify why an SDK behaves a certain way or how to handle edge cases.

- **SDK Documentation:** Each language-specific SDK should come with its own comprehensive documentation. This is your primary guide for practical, day-to-day implementation work.
    - **What's Inside:** Good SDK documentation will include: detailed installation steps, easy-to-follow quick-start guides, practical code examples (ranging from basic "hello world" setups to implementing complex Tools or Resource providers), and crucially, a detailed API reference. This reference lists all the classes, functions, methods, and configuration options provided by the SDK, explaining their parameters, return types, and behavior.
    - **Why It's Essential:** The SDK documentation translates the abstract rules of the protocol specification into concrete, actionable code constructs for your specific programming language. While different language SDKs adhere to the same MCP specification, their internal structure, class names, and helper functions might differ to feel idiomatic within their respective ecosystems. Therefore, consulting the documentation for the *specific SDK version* you are using is critical.

Treat the specification as the unchanging architectural blueprint of the city, and the SDK documentation as the detailed street map and user manual for navigating it with your specific vehicle (your chosen programming language).

Joining the Conversation: Development Resources and Community

Embarking on development with a new protocol or framework is rarely a solo journey. Leveraging the available resources and engaging with the MCP community can significantly accelerate your learning, help you overcome obstacles, and introduce you to best practices.

- **Official Documentation Portal:** This is your central hub and should be bookmarked. A well-maintained portal will consolidate everything you need: links to the latest specification, pointers to the official SDKs for all supported languages, comprehensive SDK documentation, tutorials, conceptual guides, and potentially example applications. Look for features like good organization and search functionality. (Imagine a hypothetical mcp-protocol.dev or similar).
- **Community Forums:** Seek out official forums, mailing lists, or dedicated discussion boards (like Discourse, Google Groups, etc.). These asynchronous platforms are excellent places to ask detailed questions that might require thoughtful answers, share your project experiences, discuss potential feature requests, and learn from the challenges and solutions posted by other developers.
- **Chat Channels:** For more immediate interaction, look for real-time chat communities, often hosted on platforms like Discord or Slack. These channels are great for asking quick questions, getting rapid feedback, clarifying documentation

points, and connecting informally with fellow developers and sometimes even members of the core MCP development team.

- **Code Repositories (e.g., GitHub):** The source code for the official SDKs, and possibly the specification itself, is often hosted publicly (commonly on GitHub). This transparency allows you to delve into the implementation details if needed, report bugs or issues directly, track development progress, and understand how the code works under the hood. If you're interested in contributing, look for CONTRIBUTING.md files outlining the process.

- **Examples and Tutorials:** Beyond the initial quick-start guides, actively look for more extensive examples, tutorials, or blog posts created by the core team or the community. These often demonstrate how to tackle specific real-world use cases, integrate MCP with other frameworks, or implement best practices for security and efficiency. Examples might range from simple code snippets to fully functional demo applications.

Get Involved: Don't be hesitant! Asking questions (after checking if they've been answered before) on forums or reporting issues you encounter with SDKs is incredibly valuable. Community feedback is essential for identifying bugs, improving documentation clarity, and ultimately making the Model Context Protocol ecosystem stronger and more useful for everyone. Your participation helps shape the future of MCP.

With your development environment configured, the necessary SDK installed, and a clear understanding of where to find the specification, documentation, and community support, you are now fully equipped to start coding! The next chapter will guide you through creating your first simple MCP application, allowing you to put these foundational tools and concepts into tangible practice. Let's start building the future of AI integration, together!

CHAPTER 6

Building Your First MCP Server: A Step-by-Step Guide

Welcome to the workshop! Having set up your development environment in the previous chapter, you're now ready for the exciting part: building your first MCP component. We'll start with the **MCP Server** – the part of your application that listens for requests from an AI model (acting as the MCP Client) and provides access to the Tools and Resources you define.

Think of the MCP Server as the helpful assistant sitting within your application, waiting for instructions or information requests from the AI. Building this server involves defining what capabilities it offers and implementing the logic to fulfill requests related to those capabilities.

This chapter provides a step-by-step guide to creating a simple MCP Server. We'll cover:

1. **Choosing Your Language:** Selecting the right programming language and SDK.
2. **Defining Capabilities:** Specifying the Tools, Resources, and Prompts your server will offer.
3. **Implementing Server Logic:** Writing the code to handle incoming MCP messages.
4. **Connecting to Systems:** Linking your server logic to actual data or functions.
5. **Error Handling & Logging:** Adding basic robustness and observability.

We'll use simplified pseudocode examples throughout to illustrate the concepts, which you can adapt to your chosen language using the SDKs discussed in Chapter 5. Let's begin!

Step 1: Choosing Your Programming Language (and SDK)

Before writing code, you need to decide which language you'll use for your server. Consider these factors:

- **Team Familiarity:** Use a language your team is comfortable and productive with.
- **Existing Codebase:** If integrating MCP into an existing application, using the same language is often easiest.
- **Performance Needs:** While MCP itself is lightweight, the tasks your Tools perform might have performance implications influencing language choice.
- **SDK Availability:** Ensure an official or well-supported MCP SDK exists for your chosen language (refer back to Chapter 5).

For this guide, we'll assume you've selected a language and installed the corresponding MCP SDK.

Step 2: Defining Server Capabilities (Tools, Resources, Prompts)

This is where you tell the MCP world what your server can do. You need to clearly define the Tools (actions the AI can ask your server to perform) and Resources (information the AI can request from your server). Prompts, while often user-controlled, might also be defined or managed server-side in some architectures.

These definitions are crucial because the AI model (Client) will use them to understand how to interact with your server. Definitions typically involve specifying:

- **Name:** A unique identifier (e.g., get_weather, user_preferences).
- **Description:** A clear, human-readable explanation of what the Tool/Resource does (the AI uses this!).
- **Parameters (for Tools):** The inputs the Tool requires (e.g., location for get_weather).
- **Schema (for Resources/Tool Output):** The structure of the data returned.

How you define these might vary by SDK, often involving configuration files (like YAML or JSON) or directly in your code using SDK constructs.

Pseudocode Example: Defining a Tool

```
ToolDefinition(
  name: "get_weather",
  description: "Fetches the current weather for a specified location.",
  parameters: {
   "location": { type: "string", description: "The city and state/country, e.g., London, UK" }
  },
  output_schema: {
   "temperature": { type: "number", description: "Temperature in Celsius" },
   "condition": { type: "string", description: "Weather condition, e.g., Sunny, Rainy" }
  }
)
```

Pseudocode Example: Defining a Resource

```
ResourceDefinition(
  name: "user_preferences",
  description: "Retrieves the current user's application
preferences.",
  schema: {
    "theme": { type: "string", description: "UI theme, e.g., dark,
light" },
    "notifications_enabled": { type: "boolean", description:
"Whether notifications are on" }
  }
)
```

Make these definitions clear and accurate – the AI relies
entirely on them!

Step 3: Implementing the MCP Server Logic

Now, let's write the core logic that listens for and
responds to MCP messages. The specifics depend heavily
on your chosen transport (stdio or HTTP/SSE) and SDK.

General Flow:

1. **Initialization:** Start your server application and
   initialize the MCP SDK, providing the Tool and
   Resource definitions you created.
2. **Listening:** Begin listening for incoming MCP
   messages.
   - stdio: The SDK will likely handle reading
     from standard input.
   - **HTTP/SSE:** You'll need to set up an
     HTTP server. The SDK might provide
     handlers for specific endpoints (e.g.,
     /mcp/sse for establishing the event stream,
     /mcp/message for receiving client requests if
     not using bidirectional streams).
3. **Message Handling:** When a message arrives:

o   The SDK parses the message, identifying if it's a ToolRequest, ResourceRequest, etc.
o   Based on the request (e.g., a request to use the get_weather Tool), your server dispatches the request to the appropriate handler function you've written.

Pseudocode Example: Basic Server Request Handling

```
// Initialize MCP Server with defined Tools & Resources
mcp_server = MCP.Server(tools=[get_weather_tool],
resources=[user_prefs_resource])

// Start listening (details depend on transport)
mcp_server.start_listening()

// Callback function invoked by SDK when a message arrives
function handle_incoming_request(request):
  if request.type == "ToolRequest":
   if request.tool_name == "get_weather":
    // Call the specific function that implements the get_weather
tool
     result = execute_get_weather_tool(request.parameters)
     mcp_server.send_tool_response(request.id, result)
    else:
     mcp_server.send_error_response(request.id, "Unknown
Tool")

  elif request.type == "ResourceRequest":
   if request.resource_name == "user_preferences":
    // Call the function that retrieves user preferences
    data = retrieve_user_preferences()
    mcp_server.send_resource_response(request.id, data)
    else:
     mcp_server.send_error_response(request.id, "Unknown
Resource")

  // ... handle other message types ...
```

```
// Register the handler with the SDK
mcp_server.register_request_handler(handle_incoming_request
)
```

The SDK often simplifies this, allowing you to register specific functions directly for each Tool/Resource name.

Step 4: Connecting Your Server to External Data Sources or Tools

The handler functions (like execute_get_weather_tool or retrieve_user_preferences in the pseudocode above) are the bridge between the abstract MCP request and your application's actual capabilities.

This is where you implement the *real work*:

- **For Tools:** Call the relevant function or API in your application or an external service.
- **For Resources:** Query your database, read from a file, or fetch data from an internal service.

```
Pseudocode Example: Tool Handler Implementation
(get_weather)
function execute_get_weather_tool(parameters):
  location = parameters["location"]
  try:
    // Make an actual API call to an external weather service
    weather_data = external_weather_api.get(city=location)

    // Format the result according to the defined output_schema
    result = {
      "temperature": weather_data["temp_celsius"],
      "condition": weather_data["current_condition"]
    }
    return result
  except Exception as e:
```

```
    // Error handling (see Step 5)
    log_error("Failed to get weather for " + location + ": " +
str(e))
    raise MCPToolError("Could not retrieve weather data.") //
Signal error back to MCP handler
```

Pseudocode Example: Resource Handler Implementation
(user_preferences)

```
function retrieve_user_preferences():
  try:
    // Get current user ID (from session, auth token, etc.)
    user_id = get_current_user_id()

    // Query your application's database
    prefs_record = database.query("SELECT theme, notifications
FROM preferences WHERE user_id = ?", user_id)

    if prefs_record:
      // Format according to the defined schema
      return {
        "theme": prefs_record["theme"],
        "notifications_enabled": prefs_record["notifications"]
      }
    else:
      // Handle case where preferences aren't set
      return { "theme": "default", "notifications_enabled": True }
// Provide defaults
  except Exception as e:
    log_error("Failed to retrieve preferences: " + str(e))
    raise MCPResourceError("Could not retrieve user
preferences.") // Signal error
```

Keep your MCP handling logic separate from your core
application/business logic for better organization.

Step 5: Basic Error Handling and Logging

Real-world applications encounter errors. Your MCP
server needs to handle them gracefully.

- **Error Handling:** Wrap the code in your handler functions (Step 4) in try...catch blocks (or your language's equivalent). If an error occurs (e.g., an external API is down, database query fails), catch the exception. Instead of crashing, your handler should signal an error back to the main MCP logic (Step 3), which can then send a proper MCP error response to the Client. SDKs often provide specific exception types (like MCPToolError) for this.
- **Logging:** Implement logging throughout your server. Log incoming requests, the parameters received, whether operations succeeded or failed, and any errors encountered. This is invaluable for debugging issues reported by users or observed during monitoring.

Pseudocode Example: Error Handling within Tool Handler (from Step 4)

```
function execute_get_weather_tool(parameters):
  location = parameters["location"]
  log_info("Executing get_weather tool for location: " +
location) // Logging
  try:
    weather_data = external_weather_api.get(city=location)
    result = { ... } // Format result
    log_info("Successfully retrieved weather for " + location) //
Logging success
    return result
  except APIConnectionError as e: // Specific error type
    log_error("API connection error for " + location + ": " +
str(e)) // Log specific error
    raise MCPToolError("Weather service unavailable.") //
Raise MCP-specific error
  except Exception as e: // Generic fallback
    log_error("Generic error getting weather for " + location + ":
" + str(e)) // Log generic error
```

```
raise MCPToolError("An unexpected error occurred while
retrieving weather.") // Raise MCP-specific error
```

Robust error handling and informative logging make your
server much more reliable and maintainable.

Congratulations! By following these steps, you've
outlined the structure and logic for a basic MCP Server.
You've defined its capabilities, implemented handlers to
execute requests, connected those handlers to real
functionality, and added essential error handling and
logging.

While simple, this forms the foundation upon which you
can build much more complex and powerful AI
integrations. In the next chapter, we'll look at the other
side of the coin: building an MCP Client to interact with a
server like the one you just designed.

CHAPTER 7

Building Your First MCP Client: Connecting Your AI Application

In the last chapter, we constructed an MCP Server, enabling an application to expose its unique functions (Tools) and data (Resources) in a standardized way. Now, we'll build its counterpart: the **MCP Client**. This client component lives within the application that *uses* the AI model (or perhaps contains the model itself) and is responsible for initiating communication with an MCP Server to invoke those Tools and access those Resources.

Think of the MCP Client as the AI's or application's agent, tasked with reaching out to specialized service providers (MCP Servers) to get things done or retrieve necessary information. Whether you're building a sophisticated chatbot that needs to book appointments, an IDE plugin that leverages an AI coding assistant's refactoring tools, or any other AI-enhanced application, the MCP Client is your bridge to external capabilities.

This chapter provides a practical guide to building a basic MCP Client. We'll cover:

1. **Integrating the Client:** Understanding where the client fits within your AI application.
2. **Establishing Connection:** Connecting your client to an MCP Server.
3. **Discovering Capabilities:** Learning what Tools and Resources the connected server offers.
4. **Invoking Tools & Accessing Resources:** Sending requests from your client to the server.
5. **Handling Responses:** Processing the server's replies and using the results.

As before, we'll use simplified pseudocode examples adaptable to your chosen language and MCP SDK. Let's connect your AI application!

Step 1: Integrating the MCP Client into Your Application

Where does the MCP Client logic reside? It depends on your application's architecture:

- **Chatbot Backend:** If you have a chatbot powered by an AI model, the MCP Client often lives in the backend service that orchestrates the conversation. When the AI model indicates it needs to use a tool (e.g., "I should check the user's calendar"), the backend uses the MCP Client to call the appropriate Tool on a connected MCP Server (perhaps a calendar service).
- **IDE Plugin:** In an Integrated Development Environment (IDE) with an AI coding assistant, the plugin itself might contain the MCP Client. When the user asks the assistant to refactor code, the plugin (Client) sends a ToolRequest to the AI assistant model (which might be running locally or remotely as an MCP Server exposing a refactor_code Tool).
- **Standalone Application:** An application directly embedding an AI model might also include an MCP Client to allow the model to interact with other parts of the application or external services exposed via MCP Servers.

The key is that the Client is part of the system component that needs to *initiate* requests for Tools or Resources based on the AI's reasoning or the application's workflow.

Step 2: Establishing the Connection with an MCP Server

Just like the Server, the Client needs to be initialized using the appropriate SDK and then connect using the correct transport mechanism.

1. **Initialization:** Instantiate the MCP Client object using your chosen SDK.
2. **Connection:**
   - stdio: If the Server runs locally and uses stdio, the Client process typically *starts* the Server process. The SDK then helps manage communication by attaching to the Server process's standard input and output streams.
   - **HTTP/SSE:** If the Server is remote or uses HTTP/SSE, the Client makes an initial HTTP request to the Server's designated MCP endpoint (e.g., http://server-address/mcp/sse). The Server keeps this connection open for Server-Sent Events. The SDK usually handles the complexities of managing this connection and sending subsequent messages (often via separate POST requests if needed).

Pseudocode Example: Initializing and Connecting a Client

```
// Import the MCP Client library
import MCP from 'mcp-sdk-library'; // Hypothetical library

// --- stdio Example ---
// Specify the command to start the server process
server_command = "python /path/to/mcp_server.py";
```

```
mcp_client_stdio = MCP.Client(transport="stdio",
command=server_command);
try:
  mcp_client_stdio.connect(); // Starts the server and connects
  log_info("MCP Client connected via stdio.");
except ConnectionError as e:
  log_error("Failed to connect via stdio: " + str(e));

// --- HTTP/SSE Example ---
server_url = "http://my-mcp-server.example.com/mcp"; // Base
URL for MCP endpoint
mcp_client_sse = MCP.Client(transport="sse", url=server_url);
try:
  mcp_client_sse.connect(); // Connects to the SSE endpoint
  log_info("MCP Client connected via SSE.");
except ConnectionError as e:
  log_error("Failed to connect via SSE: " + str(e));
```

A successful connection establishes the communication channel for sending requests and receiving responses.

Step 3: Discovering Server Capabilities

Once connected, how does the Client know what the Server can actually do? There are a few possibilities, often handled by the SDK:

- **Pre-configuration:** You might configure the Client with the expected list of Tools and Resources available on the specific Server it's connecting to.
- **Implicit Discovery:** The SDK might automatically request the Server's capabilities upon successful connection and make them available to your client code.
- **Explicit Discovery:** Less common, but MCP could define a specific message type for the Client to request capabilities explicitly.

Assuming the SDK handles discovery implicitly or you pre-configure, your client code needs a way to access these definitions. This is vital because the AI model often needs this list to decide *which* Tool is appropriate for a given task.

Pseudocode Example: Accessing Discovered Capabilities

```
// Assuming mcp_client is connected (stdio or sse)
try:
    // SDK might provide a method to get available
tools/resources
    available_tools = mcp_client.get_available_tools();
    available_resources = mcp_client.get_available_resources();

    log_info("Available Tools: " + str(available_tools.keys()));
    log_info("Available Resources: " +
str(available_resources.keys()));

    // Store or pass these definitions to the AI model or application
logic
    ai_context.update_available_tools(available_tools);

except Exception as e:
    log_error("Failed to retrieve server capabilities: " + str(e));
```

Knowing the available Tools and Resources allows the AI or application to make informed requests.

Step 4: Invoking Tools and Accessing Resources

This is the core function of the Client. When your application logic or AI model determines a need:

1. **Identify Target:** Determine the name of the Tool or Resource required (e.g., get_weather).

2. **Construct Message:** Create an MCP ToolRequest
   or ResourceRequest message.
   ○ For Tools, include the required parameters
     (e.g., {"location": "Paris, France"}).
   ○ For Resources, include the name.
3. **Send Message:** Use the MCP Client SDK to send
   the constructed message over the established
   connection. The SDK handles formatting and
   transmission via the chosen transport.

Pseudocode Example: Sending a Tool Request

```
// Assuming mcp_client is connected and 'get_weather' tool is
available

tool_name = "get_weather";
parameters = {"location": "Tokyo, Japan"};

try:
  log_info(f"Sending ToolRequest for '{tool_name}' with
params: {parameters}");
  // The SDK likely returns a request ID or future/promise for
tracking the response
  request_id = mcp_client.send_tool_request(tool_name,
parameters);
  log_info(f"ToolRequest sent with ID: {request_id}");

except InvalidToolError:
  log_error(f"Tool '{tool_name}' is not available on the
server.");
except ConnectionError:
  log_error("Connection lost while sending request.");
except Exception as e:
  log_error(f"Failed to send ToolRequest: {str(e)}");
```

Sending a ResourceRequest would follow a similar pattern,
just providing the resource name instead of parameters.

Step 5: Handling Responses from the Server

After sending a request, the Client must listen for and process the Server's response. This is often handled via callbacks or asynchronous event listeners provided by the SDK.

1. **Listen:** The Client continuously listens on the connection (stdio stdout or the SSE stream).
2. **Parse:** When a message arrives, the SDK parses it.
3. **Dispatch:** The SDK or your code routes the response based on its type and potentially its correlation ID (matching it to the original request).
4. **Process:**
   - ToolResponse: Extract the result data. Provide this data back to the AI model or application logic that initiated the request.
   - ResourceResponse: Extract the resource data. Update the application state or provide the data to the AI.
   - ErrorResponse: Log the error details. Inform the AI or user that the requested action failed, potentially with the reason provided in the error message.

Pseudocode Example: Basic Response Handling Callback

```
// Callback function registered with the SDK to handle
incoming messages
function handle_server_response(response):
  log_info(f"Received response (type: {response.type}, id:
{response.correlation_id})");
```

```
if response.type == "ToolResponse":
  // Find the part of the application waiting for this response
ID
  originating_request =
find_waiting_request(response.correlation_id);
  if originating_request:
    log_info(f"Tool '{originating_request.tool_name}'
succeeded. Result: {response.result}");
    // Provide result back to the AI or application logic
    ai_context.provide_tool_result(response.correlation_id,
response.result);
  else:
    log_warn(f"Received ToolResponse for unknown request
ID: {response.correlation_id}");

elif response.type == "ResourceResponse":
  originating_request =
find_waiting_request(response.correlation_id);
  if originating_request:
    log_info(f"Resource '{originating_request.resource_name}'
retrieved. Data: {response.data}");
    // Update application state or provide data to AI
    application_state.update_with_resource(originating_request.
resource_name, response.data);
  else:
    log_warn(f"Received ResourceResponse for unknown
request ID: {response.correlation_id}");

elif response.type == "ErrorResponse":
  originating_request =
find_waiting_request(response.correlation_id);
  log_error(f"Request {response.correlation_id} failed. Error:
{response.error_message}");
  if originating_request:
    // Inform AI or user about the failure
    ai_context.notify_request_failed(response.correlation_id,
response.error_message);
  else:
    log_warn(f"Received ErrorResponse for unknown request
ID: {response.correlation_id}");
```

```
// ... handle other potential message types from the server ...

// Register the handler with the client SDK
mcp_client.register_response_handler(handle_server_response);
```

Effectively handling responses closes the loop, allowing your application to utilize the results of the MCP interactions.

You've now walked through the essential steps of building an MCP Client! By integrating the client, establishing connections, discovering capabilities, sending requests, and handling responses, you can empower your AI applications to interact seamlessly with MCP Servers, unlocking a world of extended functionality. Together, the Client and Server form a powerful duo for building modular and capable AI systems.

CHAPTER 8

Working with Tools in Detail: Enabling AI Actions

In previous chapters, we introduced Tools as the mechanism by which an AI model, guided by an MCP Client, can request actions from an MCP Server. They are the verbs in the MCP sentence, allowing AI to move beyond passive observation and actively participate in workflows, interact with systems, and achieve concrete outcomes. But simply creating *a* tool isn't enough; creating *effective* tools requires careful thought and design.

This chapter delves into the nuances of working with Tools. We'll explore how to design them for maximum utility and security, how to precisely define their capabilities and limitations, how these definitions bridge the gap to modern Large Language Models (LLMs), and the best practices for implementing and testing the underlying logic. Mastering Tool design is key to unlocking reliable and powerful AI-driven actions.

Let's refine our understanding of these crucial building blocks:

1. **Designing Effective and Secure Tools:** Crafting tools that are useful, clear, and safe.
2. **Defining the Tool Blueprint:** Specifying parameters, outputs, constraints, and limitations.
3. **Bridging the Gap: LLM Compatibility:** Connecting MCP Tools to AI model function calling.
4. **Best Practices:** Implementing and testing Tool logic for robustness.

Section 1: Designing Effective and Secure Tools

Not all tools are created equal. A well-designed tool is intuitive for the AI to use, performs a valuable function, and operates within safe boundaries.

- **Usefulness & Scope:** Aim for tools that perform a specific, meaningful action. Avoid tools that are overly broad (e.g., do_everything_with_document) or too trivial. A good tool often maps to a single logical operation or API call.
    - *Analogy:* Think of a toolbox. You have specific wrenches for specific bolt sizes, not a single, vague "fix-it" tool that's hard to use precisely. A send_email tool is better than a generic communicate tool.
- **Clarity:** The Tool's name and description are critical. The AI model uses the description to understand *when* and *why* to use the tool. It must be clear, unambiguous, and accurately reflect the tool's function and any key limitations. Write descriptions *for the AI.*
    - *Example:* Instead of "Updates user," use "Updates the specified user's profile information like name or email. Requires user ID."
- **Security:** This is paramount, especially for tools that modify data or interact with external systems.
    - **Least Privilege:** Design tools to perform only the necessary actions. Don't grant excessive permissions.
    - **Input Validation:** Rigorously validate all parameters received in a ToolRequest within your server-side implementation *before* acting on them. Sanitize inputs to prevent injection attacks or unexpected behavior.

- Context Awareness: Consider the user context. Should this tool only be available to administrators? Does it operate only on the user's own data? Your MCP Server implementation needs to enforce these rules, potentially based on authentication/authorization information associated with the MCP connection or request context.
- Sensitive Data: Be cautious about what data a tool accepts as input and what it returns as output. Avoid exposing sensitive information unnecessarily.
- *Analogy:* When giving a parking valet your car key (the Tool), you ensure it only starts the car and doesn't also unlock your house or provide access to the glove compartment contents unless explicitly intended.

Section 2: Defining the Tool Blueprint: Parameters, Outputs, Constraints

As introduced in Chapter 6, the Tool Definition is the formal contract between the Server and the Client (and the AI model). Precision here prevents misunderstandings and errors.

- **Parameters (Inputs):** Define *exactly* what information the tool needs to operate.
  - **Name:** Clear, descriptive parameter names (e.g., userId, emailSubject).
  - **Type:** Specify the data type (string, number, boolean, array, object). Use specific formats where applicable (e.g., ISO 8601 date string).

- ○ **Description:** Explain what the parameter represents and any formatting rules. Crucial for the AI!
- ○ **Required/Optional:** Clearly indicate if a parameter is mandatory for the tool to function.
- ○ *Example (send_email Tool):*
  - ▪ recipient_email (string, required): "The primary recipient's email address."
  - ▪ subject (string, required): "The subject line of the email."
  - ▪ body (string, required): "The plain text content of the email."
  - ▪ cc_emails (array of strings, optional): "List of email addresses for CC recipients."
- **Outputs (Results):** Define the structure and data types of the information the tool will return upon successful execution using a clear schema. This helps the Client/AI parse and use the result.
  - ○ *Example (send_email Tool Output):*
    - ▪ status (string): "Success" or "Failed"
    - ▪ message_id (string, optional): "The unique ID of the sent email, if available."
    - ▪ error_message (string, optional): "Details if status is Failed."
- **Constraints and Limitations:** How do you communicate non-functional aspects? While the MCP specification might evolve, common approaches include:
  - ○ **In the Description:** Add critical constraints directly to the main tool description (e.g., "Fetches user profile. Requires 'read_profile' permission.").

- Custom Fields (Hypothetical): An MCP implementation or SDK *could* potentially allow adding custom metadata fields to definitions for things like permissions, rate limits, or operational notes, although this depends on the specific MCP standards you're adhering to.
- *Examples of Constraints:* Required permissions, rate limits (e.g., "Max 10 calls per minute"), data scope (e.g., "Only operates on data created by the current user"), cost implications.

Section 3: Bridging the Gap: LLM Compatibility (Function Calling)

One of the most powerful applications of MCP is enabling Large Language Models (LLMs) to use tools. Modern LLMs (from OpenAI, Google, Anthropic, etc.) often support "Function Calling" or "Tool Use," where the model can indicate its intent to call an external function and provide the necessary arguments.

The good news is that the structured way MCP requires you to define Tools (name, description, parameter schema, output schema) maps almost perfectly to the JSON Schema format these LLMs typically expect for their function/tool definitions.

- **The Connection:** The name, description, and parameter definitions (including types, descriptions, required status) from your MCP Tool Definition can be directly translated into the JSON structure the LLM needs to understand your tool.
- **SDK Support:** A well-designed MCP SDK might even provide utility functions to automatically

generate the LLM-compatible JSON schema directly from your native MCP Tool Definitions. This simplifies integration significantly.

1. *Example:*
   mcp_tool_definition.to_openai_json_schema()
   or
   mcp_tool_definition.to_google_ai_function_decl aration().

- **The Flow:**
  1. You provide the LLM with the list of available MCP Tools, formatted in its required JSON schema.
  2. During conversation, the LLM decides to use a tool (e.g., get_weather).
  3. The LLM's response includes a special indicator and the arguments (e.g., {"location": "London, UK"}).
  4. Your application backend (containing the MCP Client) receives this.
  5. The MCP Client constructs and sends the ToolRequest to the appropriate MCP Server.
  6. The Server executes the tool and sends back a ToolResponse.
  7. The Client receives the response and feeds the result back into the LLM conversation context.
  8. The LLM uses the tool's result to formulate its final answer to the user.

- *Analogy:* Your MCP Tool Definition is like a universal blueprint written in a standard engineering language. The SDK acts as a translator, converting that blueprint into the specific dialect (JSON schema) that your chosen LLM architect understands, allowing them to incorporate your tool into their plans.

Section 4: Best Practices for Implementation and Testing

Defining a tool is only half the battle; implementing the server-side logic robustly and testing it thoroughly is crucial for reliability.

- **Implementation Best Practices:**
    - **Robust Error Handling:** Wrap your core tool logic in try...catch blocks. Handle expected errors gracefully (e.g., API timeouts, invalid inputs, permission denied) and return informative MCP error responses via your server logic. Don't let internal exceptions crash the whole server.
    - **Idempotency:** Where possible and appropriate, design tools to be idempotent. This means calling the tool multiple times with the exact same parameters should produce the same result or system state as calling it once. This is vital for safely retrying requests in case of network issues. (e.g., set_user_preference(theme='dark') is idempotent, while toggle_notification() is not). Clearly document whether a tool is idempotent.
    - **Separation of Concerns:** Isolate your core business logic/API interaction code from the MCP-specific request/response handling code. This makes your code cleaner, easier to test, and reusable.
    - **Manage Dependencies:** Properly handle connections to databases, external APIs, or other services your tool relies on. Use connection pooling, handle timeouts, and manage credentials securely.

- o **Logging:** Log key information within your tool implementation: received parameters, significant steps, success/failure outcomes, and detailed error information.
- **Testing Strategies:**
  - o **Unit Tests:** Test the core logic of your tool function in isolation. Use mocking frameworks to simulate dependencies (databases, external APIs) and verify the logic under various conditions (success, different inputs, expected errors).
  - o **Integration Tests:** Test the tool end-to-end through the MCP Server. Send actual ToolRequest messages (using an MCP client test harness or SDK) and verify that the correct ToolResponse or ErrorResponse is returned via the MCP transport.
  - o **Edge Case Testing:** Explicitly test for boundary conditions: invalid parameter types, missing required parameters, parameters with unexpected values, simulated failures from dependencies, permission errors.
  - o **Security Testing:** Consider tests for potential vulnerabilities, especially if the tool handles sensitive data or performs critical actions (e.g., testing input sanitization).

Well-designed, clearly defined, securely implemented, and thoroughly tested Tools are the bedrock of effective AI action-taking via MCP. By investing care in their creation, you build a reliable bridge between the reasoning capabilities of AI models and the practical functions of your applications and services. This detailed approach ensures your AI integrations are not just powerful, but also predictable and safe.

CHAPTER 9

Leveraging Resources and Prompts for Enhanced Context

In the previous chapter, we took a deep dive into MCP Tools, the components that allow AI models to perform actions. However, actions rarely happen in a vacuum. For an AI to act intelligently, it needs **context**. It needs access to relevant information (What's the user's name? What's in the shopping cart? What's the status of the project?), and it often benefits from guidance on *how* to approach a specific task. This is where MCP **Resources** and **Prompts** shine.

While Tools are the "verbs," Resources are the "nouns" – providing access to application-controlled data – and Prompts are the "stage directions" – guiding the AI's performance for optimal results. Mastering the use of Resources and Prompts is crucial for moving beyond simple command-execution and building AI integrations that are deeply aware of their environment and purpose.

This chapter will guide you through:

1. **Making Data Accessible:** Exposing application-controlled data effectively as MCP Resources.
2. **Guiding Interactions:** Designing and utilizing user-controlled Prompts for optimized AI communication.
3. **Effective Context Management:** Strategies for combining Resources, Prompts, and Tools for truly context-aware AI.

Let's explore how to enrich your AI's understanding and guide its interactions.

Section 1: Unlocking Application Data with Resources

Resources are the windows through which the AI model (via the MCP Client) can view relevant information managed by your application (the MCP Server). They provide controlled, typically read-only access to the data the AI needs to understand the current state of affairs.

- **What Makes a Good Resource?**
  - **Relevance:** Expose data that is genuinely useful for the AI's tasks (e.g., user profiles, product catalogs, document contents, application settings, sensor readings, database records).
  - **Accuracy:** The MCP Server is responsible for ensuring the data provided through a Resource is up-to-date and accurate. Stale or incorrect information leads to poor AI decisions.
  - **Security:** Access control is critical. The Server *must* enforce permissions, ensuring the Client/AI only receives data it's authorized to see based on the user context or connection credentials. Don't expose sensitive data unnecessarily.
- **Designing Resource Granularity:** How much data should a single Resource provide?
  - **Too Broad:** A single massive application_state Resource might be easy to define but inefficient to fetch and hard for the AI to parse for specific information.
  - **Too Narrow:** Hundreds of tiny Resources might become difficult to manage and discover.
  - **Just Right:** Aim for logical groupings. For instance, instead of one user_data blob,

consider separate Resources like user_profile (name, email), user_settings (theme, notifications), and user_activity_log (recent actions).

- o *Analogy:* Think of organizing a filing cabinet. You wouldn't put every document into one giant drawer (too broad), nor would you create a separate folder for every single sentence (too narrow). You create logically grouped folders (like user_profile, user_settings).
- **Defining Resources:** Similar to Tools, Resources need clear definitions:
  - o **Name:** A unique identifier (e.g., product_inventory, current_document_text).
  - o **Description:** A clear explanation for the AI about what data this Resource provides.
  - o **Schema:** Defines the structure and data types of the information returned.
  - o *Pseudocode Example (product_inventory Resource):*

```
ResourceDefinition(
  name: "product_inventory",
  description: "Retrieves current stock levels for specified
product SKUs.",
  # Note: Parameters might be passed in ResourceRequest, or
implied by context
  # For simplicity, let's assume it returns data for relevant SKUs
based on context
  schema: {
    type: "array",
    items: {
      type: "object",
      properties: {
        "sku": { type: "string", description: "Product Stock
```

Keeping Unit" },
        "stock_level": { type: "integer", description: "Current
number of units in stock" },
        "status": { type: "string", description: "e.g., In Stock, Low
Stock, Out of Stock" }
      }
    }
  }
)

○

- **Implementation Considerations:**
  - ○ **Server-Side Logic:** The MCP Server code
    implements the logic to fetch the data
    (from databases, APIs, internal state) when
    a Resource is requested, ensuring security
    checks are performed.
  - ○ **Caching:** For frequently accessed
    Resources where data doesn't change
    constantly, consider implementing caching
    on the server-side to improve performance
    and reduce load on underlying data
    sources.

Resources provide the essential *data context*, grounding
the AI's understanding in the reality of your application's
state.

Section 2: Guiding the AI with Prompts

If Resources provide the "what," Prompts help define the
"how." Prompts are structured templates or instructions,
typically controlled by the user or developer, designed to
guide the AI's interaction for specific tasks, ensuring
consistency and optimizing performance.

- **Why Use Prompts?**
  - **Consistency:** Ensure recurring tasks are handled similarly each time.
  - **Optimization:** Tailor instructions to get the best possible output from the AI for a specific task (e.g., summarization style, email tone).
  - **Clarity:** Reduce ambiguity in user requests by providing a clear structure.
  - **Efficiency:** Ensure the AI asks for or receives all necessary information upfront, reducing back-and-forth clarification.
- **Designing Effective Prompts:**
  - **Clear Instructions:** Use direct language. Tell the AI its role, the task, the desired output format, and any constraints.
  - **Placeholders:** Use placeholders (e.g., [document_text], [user_name], [recipient_email]) for dynamic data that will be filled in at runtime, often using data retrieved via Resources.
  - **Contextual Information:** Include relevant context directly in the prompt or reference Resources the AI should consult.
  - **Output Formatting:** Specify the desired output structure (e.g., "Provide a JSON object with keys 'summary' and 'keywords'," "Write a bulleted list").
  - *Analogy:* A well-designed prompt is like a detailed recipe or a fill-in-the-blanks form. It guides the user (or AI) step-by-step, ensuring all necessary ingredients (information) are included and the final dish (output) meets expectations.
- **Example Prompts:**
  - *Summarization Task:*

*   *   *Role:* * You are a helpful assistant tasked with summarizing documents.*
*   *   *Context:* * The document content is provided below, retrieved using the 'document_content' Resource.*
*   *   *Task:* * Provide a concise summary (max 3 sentences) focusing on the main conclusions.*
*   *   *Document Content:* * [placeholder_for_document_text]*
*   *   *Output:* *

Summary: [Your concise summary here]

o   *Email Drafting Task:*

*   *   *Role:* * You are drafting a professional email.*
*   *   *Context:* * Use the 'user_profile' Resource to get the sender's name for the signature. The recipient email is [recipient_email_placeholder].*
*   *   *Task:* * Draft an email with the subject line "[subject_placeholder]". The body should politely follow up on the meeting about "[topic_placeholder]" and mention that notes are attached. Keep the tone professional and friendly.*
*   *   *Output:* *

To: [recipient_email_placeholder]
Subject: [subject_placeholder]
Body: [Your drafted email body here]

Best regards,
[sender_name_from_user_profile]

o

*   **Managing Prompts:** Prompts can be managed in various ways:
    o   **Hardcoded:** Defined directly in the application code (simple, less flexible).

- Configuration Files: Stored alongside application settings (better flexibility).
- User Settings: Allow users to customize prompts for their specific needs.
- Prompt Management Systems: Dedicated systems for creating, versioning, and deploying prompts, especially in complex applications.

Prompts provide crucial *task context* and *interaction guidance*, helping the AI perform specific operations more effectively and consistently.

Section 3: Strategies for Effective Context Management

The true power of MCP emerges when you strategically combine Tools, Resources, and Prompts to manage the overall context available to the AI. Effective context management leads to AI interactions that are more relevant, accurate, and efficient.

- **Types of Context in MCP:**
  - **Capability Context:** Provided by the definitions of available Tools and Resources. The AI knows *what* it *can* potentially do or know.
  - **Data Context:** Provided by accessing Resources. The AI gets specific, real-time information relevant to the current situation.
  - **Task Context:** Provided by Prompts. The AI receives guidance on *how* to approach a specific task or structure its response.
  - **Conversation History:** (Implicit) The ongoing dialogue also forms part of the

context, which MCP interactions build upon.

- **Synergy in Action:** Resources, Prompts, and Tools often work together in a sequence:
  - A **Prompt** might structure the overall task for the AI.
  - The AI determines it needs specific information and requests data via one or more **Resources**.
  - The AI processes the data obtained from the Resources (potentially guided further by the Prompt).
  - The AI decides to perform an action and invokes a **Tool**, possibly using data retrieved from Resources as parameters.
  - The result from the Tool is processed, and the AI formulates its final response, potentially adhering to output formats specified in the Prompt.
- **Example Scenario Revisited:** User asks, "Summarize my latest project report and email it to Bob."
  - **Prompt (Guidance):** An internal prompt might structure this multi-step task: Find latest report -> Get content -> Summarize -> Find Bob's email -> Draft & Send.
  - **Resource (Data):** AI requests document_list Resource (filtered for "project report", sorted by date) to get the latest report ID.
  - **Resource (Data):** AI requests document_content Resource using the ID.
  - **AI Processing (Guided by Prompt):** AI summarizes the content, perhaps following specific instructions from a summarization prompt template.

- Resource (Data): AI requests contact_list Resource (filtered for "Bob") to get the email address.
  - Tool (Action): AI invokes send_email Tool, passing Bob's email (from Resource) and the generated summary.
- **Strategic Considerations:**
  - **Context Window Limits:** Be mindful of the AI model's context window size. Don't overload it by fetching excessively large Resources if only a small part is needed. Design Resources and Prompts efficiently.
  - **Information Flow:** Design the flow of information – when should Resources be fetched? How should Prompt templates incorporate Resource data? When are Tools called?
  - **User Experience:** Ensure the process feels seamless to the end-user, even if multiple MCP interactions are happening behind the scenes.

By thoughtfully providing data context through Resources and task context through Prompts, you enable the AI to utilize Tools far more effectively, leading to sophisticated, reliable, and genuinely helpful AI integrations.

Tools give AI hands, but Resources and Prompts give it eyes and a map. By mastering the interplay between these core MCP components, you move beyond simple commands towards building AI applications that possess a deeper understanding of their environment and purpose, allowing them to act with greater relevance and intelligence.

CHAPTER 10

Security Best Practices for MCP Implementations

As we've seen, the Model Context Protocol unlocks incredible potential by allowing AI models and applications to communicate and collaborate, acting as a powerful nervous system for intelligent applications. However, this very interconnectedness introduces new avenues for potential security risks. Integrating systems, handling data, and enabling automated actions requires a security-first mindset. Treating security as an afterthought is not an option; it must be woven into the fabric of your MCP design and implementation from day one, recognizing that security is a shared responsibility across all connected components.

This chapter is dedicated to navigating the security landscape of MCP. We'll identify potential threats and provide practical, actionable best practices to safeguard your applications, your data, and your users. Building trust in AI integrations, especially those capable of taking action, requires building them securely and transparently.

We will cover essential security pillars:

1. **Understanding the Threat Landscape:** Identifying potential security risks specific to MCP and their impact.
2. **Authentication & Authorization:** Securely verifying identities and permissions (using OAuth 2.1).
3. **Token Management:** Best practices for handling access credentials throughout their lifecycle.

4. **Input Validation & Sanitization:** Protecting against malicious inputs and various injection attacks.
5. **Network Security:** Securing the communication channels between MCP components.
6. **Monitoring & Logging:** Maintaining visibility and crucial audit trails for accountability and incident response.
7. **User Consent & Control:** Empowering users and respecting data privacy through transparency and choice.
8. **Least Privilege:** Applying this fundamental security principle consistently.

Let's build a secure foundation for your MCP integrations.

Section 1: Understanding the Threat Landscape

Before we can defend our system, we need to understand what we're defending against. Awareness of potential vulnerabilities is the first step towards mitigation. Common security risks in an MCP context include:

- **Token Theft/Abuse:** If an MCP Client's access token is stolen (e.g., through malware, phishing, insecure storage), an attacker could impersonate the legitimate client. *Impact:* Unauthorized access to sensitive Resource data, execution of potentially harmful Tools, financial loss, reputational damage, and violation of user trust.
- **Server Compromise:** If the MCP Server itself is compromised (e.g., via an operating system vulnerability, insecure deployment configuration), an attacker could gain deep control. *Impact:* Tampering with Tool execution logic, manipulating Resource data returned to clients,

accessing underlying application databases or systems, potentially using the server as a launchpad for further attacks within your infrastructure.

- **Insecure Tool Implementation:** Tools that don't properly validate inputs or interact insecurely with backend systems create direct vulnerabilities. *Impact:* Exploitation could lead to command injection (allowing arbitrary code execution on the server), SQL injection (data exfiltration or manipulation), Cross-Site Scripting (XSS) if tool outputs are rendered insecurely, or other application-specific flaws.
- **Data Leakage:** Resources might inadvertently expose sensitive information if access control logic on the server-side is flawed or doesn't correctly check the permissions associated with the requesting client/user context. *Impact:* Serious privacy violations, non-compliance with regulations (like GDPR or CCPA), erosion of user trust, and potential competitive disadvantage.
- **Prompt Injection:** Maliciously crafted input, often cleverly disguised within seemingly benign user requests to the AI, could trick the AI model into misusing a Tool or revealing sensitive information present in its context or prompt. *Impact:* Unpredictable and potentially harmful AI behavior, unauthorized actions via Tools (like sending emails or deleting data), exfiltration of sensitive data included in the prompt context.
- **Denial of Service (DoS):** An attacker could flood the MCP Server with a high volume of requests (valid or invalid), overwhelming its processing capacity, network bandwidth, or downstream dependencies. *Impact:* The MCP Server becomes unavailable for legitimate users and clients,

causing service disruption and potential business impact.

Analogy: Securing a connected smart home (your MCP ecosystem) requires understanding threats like someone stealing your remote control (token theft), breaking into the central control hub (server compromise), exploiting faulty wiring in a smart appliance (insecure tool), a camera streaming video publicly (data leakage), or tricking the voice assistant into unlocking the door with a cleverly phrased command (prompt injection).

Section 2: Fortifying the Gates: Authentication & Authorization (OAuth 2.1)

We need robust mechanisms to reliably verify *who* is making a request (Authentication) and *what* they are specifically allowed to do (Authorization). Simply knowing who someone is isn't enough; we need to know their permissions.

- **Recommendation:** Use industry-standard protocols. **OAuth 2.1** is the current recommended framework for delegated authorization. Relying on standards like OAuth 2.1 is crucial because they are extensively vetted by the security community, benefit from widespread library support, and promote interoperability. It provides a secure way for a Client (acting on behalf of a user or as a standalone service) to obtain limited permission (in the form of an access token) to access specific Resources or invoke specific Tools on an MCP Server.
- **Simplified Flow:**
    1. The MCP Client application directs the user (if user interaction is involved) to a

trusted Authorization Server (which might be part of your platform or a third-party identity provider).

2. The user authenticates directly with the Authorization Server (e.g., username/password, MFA). The Client never sees these primary credentials. The user then grants permission for the Client to access specific scopes (e.g., read_profile, send_email, manage_calendar).

3. The Authorization Server issues a time-limited access token (and potentially a longer-lived refresh token) back to the Client, encoding the granted scopes within the token or associated data.

4. The Client includes this access token (typically as a Bearer token in the Authorization header) in its requests to the MCP Server.

5. The MCP Server receives the request, extracts the token, and validates it cryptographically (checking its signature against the Authorization Server's public key, verifying its expiration time, and ensuring it was issued by the expected authority for the intended audience - itself). Crucially, it then checks if the validated token's granted scopes permit the specific operation being requested (e.g., accessing the user_profile Resource requires the read_profile scope). Access is denied if validation fails or scopes are insufficient.

- **Key Benefit:** This flow decouples authentication from the MCP Client and Server. The Client doesn't handle user passwords, and the Server trusts the cryptographically verifiable assertion made by the Authorization Server via the token.

Section 3: Handling Credentials Securely: Token Management

Access tokens are like temporary keys; they grant access and must be handled with extreme care throughout their lifecycle.

- **Transport Security:** *Always* transmit tokens over channels encrypted using up-to-date **TLS** configurations. Ensure your clients and servers validate TLS certificates properly to prevent man-in-the-middle attacks. Never send tokens over unencrypted HTTP.
- **Secure Storage:** Avoid storing tokens in insecure locations. Client-side browser storage (like localStorage or sessionStorage) is particularly risky as it's easily accessible via Cross-Site Scripting (XSS) attacks. Prefer secure backend session storage, platform-managed credential stores, or potentially HttpOnly cookies (for web applications, ensuring robust Cross-Site Request Forgery (CSRF) protection is also in place). Mobile applications should use platform-provided secure storage like Android Keystore or iOS Keychain.
- **Short Expiration:** Use short-lived access tokens (e.g., minutes to a few hours). The shorter the lifespan, the less time an attacker has to exploit a compromised token. This is a critical mitigation strategy.
- **Refresh Tokens:** For scenarios requiring longer user sessions, use refresh tokens. These are typically longer-lived but should be stored more securely than access tokens (e.g., backend

database, HttpOnly cookie) and are used *only* to obtain new, short-lived access tokens from the Authorization Server. Implement refresh token rotation (issuing a new refresh token with each use) for enhanced security.

- **Token Scopes:** Grant tokens the narrowest possible set of permissions (scopes) required for the specific tasks the client needs to perform. Avoid overly broad scopes. For example, differentiate between a read_calendar scope and a more powerful manage_calendar scope. This adheres to the Principle of Least Privilege.

- **Revocation:** Implement a reliable mechanism for administrators or users to revoke tokens immediately if they are suspected of being compromised (e.g., device lost, suspected breach). This often involves the Authorization Server maintaining a revocation list or providing a token introspection endpoint that the MCP Server can check.

Section 4: Sanitizing Inputs, Defending Against Injection

A fundamental security rule: **Never trust external input.** Data coming from MCP Clients, or user input relayed through an AI, must be treated as potentially hostile.

- **Server-Side Input Validation:** Rigorous validation *must* occur on the MCP Server side for all parameters received in ToolRequest messages and any context influencing ResourceRequest messages. Client-side validation is purely for user experience and can be easily bypassed. Check data types, enforce length limits, validate against expected formats (e.g., using regular expressions), check ranges for numbers, and ensure values fall

92

within allowed sets (enums). Reject any request that fails validation immediately with a clear error.

- **Sanitization & Contextual Escaping:** Before using *any* validated input data in downstream operations, sanitize it to remove potentially harmful characters or, more effectively, escape it appropriately for the specific context where it will be used. Use parameterized queries or prepared statements for database interactions (the gold standard against SQL injection). Use appropriate encoding/escaping libraries when rendering data in HTML (to prevent XSS), constructing file paths, or executing shell commands (be *extremely* careful here, avoid if possible). The correct escaping method depends entirely on the target system.

- **Prompt Injection Mitigation:** This remains a challenging and evolving area in AI security. There's no single perfect solution. A layered defense approach is recommended:
  - **Clear Delimitation:** Use distinct markers, XML tags, or structural conventions within your prompts to clearly separate your trusted instructions to the LLM from potentially untrusted user-provided input.
  - **Instructional Defense (System Prompt):** Explicitly instruct the LLM in its system prompt to be wary of user input that attempts to contradict its primary instructions, impersonate the system, or misuse tools. Tell it to prioritize its original instructions.
  - **Input/Output Filtering:** Implement filters to detect and potentially block known malicious patterns or keywords in user input before it reaches the LLM. Similarly,

filter LLM outputs before displaying them or passing them to tools, especially looking for patterns that might indicate sensitive data leakage.
- ○ **Human Oversight:** For Tools performing highly sensitive or irreversible actions (e.g., financial transactions, deleting significant data), consider implementing a workflow step that requires explicit human confirmation before the action is executed, even if initiated by the AI.

Analogy: Think of airport security: baggage is X-rayed and potentially opened for inspection (input validation/sanitization), and passengers present passports and boarding passes that are verified against official records (authentication/authorization). Multiple layers of checks are performed.

Section 5: Securing the Connection: Network Security

The communication lines between MCP Clients and Servers must be protected.

- **TLS Everywhere:** Mandate the use of strong, up-to-date TLS configurations (TLS 1.2 or preferably 1.3) for *all* MCP communication, including the SSE transport (which runs over HTTPS). This encrypts data in transit, preventing eavesdropping (confidentiality) and tampering (integrity). Ensure proper certificate management, including using trusted Certificate Authorities (CAs) and timely renewals.
- **Rate Limiting:** Implement robust rate limiting on the MCP Server's API endpoints. Configure limits

based on factors like source IP address, authenticated user/client ID, or specific API endpoints. This is crucial for mitigating DoS attacks, preventing resource exhaustion, and limiting the impact of runaway clients or brute-force attacks.

- **Timeouts:** Configure sensible network and application-level timeouts for establishing connections and waiting for responses. Overly long timeouts can tie up server resources, making it vulnerable to slowloris-style DoS attacks and degrading overall performance.

Section 6: Watching and Recording: Monitoring & Logging

Effective security requires visibility. You need to know what's happening on your MCP Server to detect, investigate, and respond to potential incidents.

- **Comprehensive Logging:** Log critical security-related events on the MCP Server with sufficient detail. Essential events include:
  - Authentication attempts (success/failure, source IP, user/client ID).
  - Authorization decisions (token validation results, granted/denied scopes for specific requests).
  - MCP requests received (timestamp, source IP, client ID, requested Tool/Resource name, *non-sensitive* parameters – **never log secrets or PII in parameters**).
  - MCP responses sent (timestamp, success/error status, correlation ID).
  - Significant internal errors during Tool execution or Resource retrieval (stack traces, error messages).

- Use structured logging formats (like JSON) to make logs easier to parse and analyze automatically. Include correlation IDs to trace a single logical operation across multiple log entries.
- **Secure Audit Trails:** Ensure logs provide a clear, chronological, and reliable record of activities. Protect log files from unauthorized access or tampering (e.g., using write-only permissions, forwarding logs to a separate secure aggregation system). Retain logs according to your organization's policy and regulatory requirements.
- **Monitoring & Alerting:** Implement automated monitoring on logs and server performance metrics. Configure alerts for suspicious patterns that could indicate an attack or malfunction, such as: high rates of authentication failures, sudden spikes in error responses, unusual request volumes from specific IPs or clients, requests targeting non-existent tools/resources, or performance degradation indicative of a DoS attack. Timely alerts enable rapid incident response.

Section 7: Empowering Users: Consent and Control

Security isn't just about protecting the system; it's also about respecting user privacy and empowering them with control over their data and how applications act on their behalf.

- **Transparency:** Be clear, concise, and upfront with users about what data your application's Resources might access and what specific actions its Tools can perform when granted permission. Provide this information in easy-to-understand language, perhaps linked directly from the consent screen during the OAuth flow.

- **Granular Consent:** Leverage OAuth scopes effectively. Allow users to grant permissions for specific categories of actions or data access, rather than demanding a single, all-encompassing permission. This builds user trust and limits the potential impact if a specific permission is misused. Examples: read_profile, read_calendar_events, add_calendar_events, send_email_on_my_behalf.
- **User Control:** Provide users with a clear interface (e.g., within their account settings) where they can easily review which applications have been granted permissions via MCP/OAuth, see the specific scopes granted, and revoke those permissions at any time. Consider offering a view of recent sensitive actions performed by AI via Tools on their behalf.

Section 8: The Golden Rule: Principle of Least Privilege

This principle is fundamental and should be applied consistently across your entire MCP implementation. Grant only the minimum necessary permissions required for a component or process to perform its intended function.

- **Server Process:** The MCP Server application itself should run under an operating system user account with the absolute minimum privileges needed to operate – avoid running as root or administrator. Limit its network access and file system permissions.
- **Tokens:** As emphasized previously, OAuth tokens requested by clients and granted by the

authorization server should be scoped to the minimum required permissions for the client's functionality. Don't request manage_everything if only read_profile is needed.

- **Tools:** When implementing the server-side logic for a Tool, ensure that the code executing the tool's action only has access to the specific backend systems, database tables/rows, APIs, or file system paths it strictly needs. For example, a tool designed to update a user's email address should only have database permissions to modify the email field in the user table for the relevant user, not permissions to delete users or access unrelated tables. Reducing the "blast radius" if a component is compromised is a key benefit.

Security in MCP is not a feature you add at the end; it's a fundamental requirement built in from the start and maintained throughout the application lifecycle. By understanding the risks and diligently applying these best practices – robust authentication/authorization using standards like OAuth 2.1, secure token handling, rigorous input validation, strong network protection, vigilant monitoring and logging, user empowerment through consent and control, and the pervasive principle of least privilege – you can build powerful, innovative AI integrations that users and organizations can trust. Remember, security is an ongoing effort, demanding continuous learning, adaptation, and vigilance as both technology and threats evolve.

CHAPTER 11

Advanced MCP Features and Concepts

Having mastered the fundamentals of MCP Clients, Servers, Tools, Resources, Prompts, and security best practices, you're now equipped to build robust AI integrations. But the Model Context Protocol offers more depth and flexibility for tackling complex scenarios where simpler request-response patterns fall short. This chapter delves into some of the advanced features and concepts that unlock even greater power and nuance, enabling more sophisticated and adaptive AI behaviors.

Think of the previous chapters as learning the standard rules and pieces of chess. Now, we'll explore advanced strategies and special moves – capabilities like server-controlled generation (Sampling), defining clear boundaries (Roots), real-time updates (Notifications), coordinating multiple AI agents, handling complex back-and-forth interactions, and streaming results for long-running tasks. These features address the limitations inherent in basic interactions and allow for truly dynamic systems.

Understanding these advanced concepts will allow you to design and implement AI systems that are more dynamic, responsive, scalable, and capable of handling intricate workflows. Let's explore the cutting edge of MCP:

1. **Exploring Sampling:** Enabling server-controlled influence over LLM completions.
2. **Understanding Roots:** Defining clear access and capability boundaries within a server.
3. **Utilizing Notifications:** Pushing real-time updates from server to client.

4. **Hierarchical Agent Systems:** Facilitating interactions between multiple MCP components.
5. **Interactive Workflows:** Managing multi-step processes and user interactions.
6. **Real-Time Streaming:** Handling results from long-running operations efficiently.

Section 1: Exploring Sampling (Server-Controlled Completions)

Typically, an AI model (often within the MCP Client application) handles the core generative tasks, deciding what text to produce based on its training and the provided prompt. However, MCP might include mechanisms for **Sampling**, where the MCP Server, possessing unique application context or business logic, can actively influence or participate in the LLM's generation process.

- **What it Might Mean:** This goes beyond simply providing data via Resources. Sampling could involve the Server sending specific parameters alongside a generation request (or perhaps via a dedicated MCP message type) that modify the LLM's sampling behavior. This might include setting parameters like temperature or top-k, providing positive/negative constraints, supplying preferred phrasing examples, dictating the use of specific terminology, or even pre-generating certain parts of the response that the LLM must incorporate. The exact mechanism would depend on the specific MCP extensions and LLM capabilities being used.
- **Potential Use Cases:**
  - **Enforcing Output Formats:** While prompts can suggest formats, Sampling could allow the Server to *enforce* strict

adherence to a complex JSON schema or structured template *during* generation, reducing the likelihood of malformed output that breaks downstream server-side processes. This catches errors earlier than client-side validation.

- o **Injecting Server-Side Logic:** Imagine an e-commerce AI assistant. Using Sampling, the Server could dynamically calculate and inject a personalized discount code or real-time shipping estimate directly into the AI's response, based on complex rules unknown to the AI model itself.
- o **Fine-Tuning Responses:** Guiding the LLM's tone (e.g., formal vs. casual), style, or specific content choices based on application state (e.g., user subscription level, recent support interactions) or A/B testing parameters managed server-side.
- o **Constrained Generation:** Forcing the LLM's output to select only from a list of currently valid options (e.g., available appointment slots, in-stock product variants) that are managed and validated by the Server in real-time.

- • **Analogy:** Imagine directing a movie. Normally, the director (Client/AI) gives the actor (LLM) general instructions. With Sampling, the director (Server) might step in during rehearsal or even during the take to provide a specific line reading (preferred phrasing), dictate a precise blocking move (output structure constraint), provide a specific prop that *must* be used (required terminology or data), or adjust the lighting (sampling parameters like temperature) to ensure the final performance perfectly aligns with the

101

director's real-time vision and the scene's requirements.

Sampling offers a powerful, albeit complex, way for the application backend (Server) to exert finer-grained, context-aware control over AI generation when simple prompting or post-processing is insufficient.

Section 2: Understanding Roots (Defining Access Boundaries)

As MCP Servers grow in complexity, potentially exposing dozens or hundreds of Tools and Resources, managing this capability landscape and controlling access becomes a significant challenge. **Roots** (a hypothetical but plausible advanced concept in MCP) could provide a structured mechanism for defining logical boundaries, namespaces, or capability subsets within a single MCP Server instance.

- **What They Might Be:** A Root could represent a specific functional domain (e.g., billing, user_management), a dataset partition (e.g., project_alpha_files), a permission level (e.g., admin_tools, read_only_data), or a combination thereof. Each Root would logically group and expose only a specific subset of the Server's total available Tools and Resources. A client might connect or authenticate *to a specific Root.*
- **Purpose:**
  - **Organization & Discovery:** Grouping related Tools and Resources makes the Server's capabilities easier for clients (and developers) to understand, discover, and navigate, especially in large systems.
  - **Granular Access Control:** Define different permission sets or access scopes

tied to specific Roots. This simplifies authorization logic compared to managing permissions individually for every single Tool and Resource. A client's token might grant access only to the reporting Root, for instance.

- o **Multi-Tenancy:** Enable a single Server deployment to securely serve multiple distinct clients, user groups, or tenants. Each tenant could interact with their own isolated Root, ensuring data privacy and preventing capability interference between tenants.
- o **Contextual Capabilities:** Dynamically expose different Roots (and thus different capabilities) to a client based on the current application state, user role, or the specific task context, providing a more tailored and relevant interface.
- **Analogy:** Think of a large university campus (MCP Server). Different colleges or major departments like Physics, Literature, Engineering, and Administration act as **Roots**. Each Root has its own specialized laboratories (Tools) and libraries (Resources). A physics undergraduate might primarily have an ID card granting access to the Physics Root facilities, while a university administrator might have access to the Administration Root. This prevents physics students from accidentally using sensitive administrative tools and keeps the capability sets relevant and manageable.

Roots could offer a powerful architectural pattern for managing complexity, enforcing robust security boundaries, and providing tailored capability sets within large-scale, multi-functional MCP Servers.

Section 3: Utilizing Notifications for Real-Time Updates

The standard MCP interaction model is primarily client-driven: the Client sends a request, and the Server sends a response. But many modern applications require the Server to inform the Client about events or state changes *proactively* and asynchronously. This is the purpose of MCP **Notifications**.

- **What They Are:** Asynchronous, server-initiated messages sent to the Client over the established MCP connection, independent of any specific prior request from the Client.
- **How They Differ:** Unlike responses, which are directly tied to a preceding request (often via a correlation ID), Notifications are pushed by the Server whenever a relevant event occurs on the backend or a state change needs to be communicated.
- **Use Cases:**
  - **External Event Alerts:** Immediately informing the Client/AI about significant external events, such as "A new email matching your filter has arrived," "Database record X related to your current task has been updated by another user," or "Inventory level for product Y just dropped below the threshold."
  - **Progress Updates:** Sending periodic updates on the status or percentage completion of a long-running Tool execution that was initiated earlier by the Client (complementary to Streaming).

104

- o **Asynchronous Operations:** Notifying the Client when a background task (perhaps triggered non-blockingly by a Tool) has successfully completed or encountered an error.
- o **Real-Time Collaboration:** In multi-user applications, notifying connected clients when another user makes a change relevant to their current view or task (e.g., editing a shared document, adding a comment).
- **Transport & Reliability:** The Server-Sent Events (SSE) transport is inherently well-suited for delivering Notifications due to its persistent server-to-client connection. Implementations might need to consider reliability aspects, such as how to handle notifications if a client briefly disconnects (e.g., using sequence numbers or requiring the client to re-sync state upon reconnection). Different notification types (e.g., informational, critical) might warrant different delivery guarantees.
- **Analogy:** Notifications are like breaking news alerts or social media updates pushed to your phone. You don't have to constantly open the app and manually refresh (send requests) to see if anything new happened; the app's server proactively tells your phone (Client) immediately when there's an important update.

Notifications transform MCP interactions from purely pull-based to potentially push-based, enabling more dynamic, event-driven, and responsive applications that react instantly to backend changes.

Section 4: Working with Hierarchical Agent Systems

The standardized nature of MCP, defining clear roles (Client/Server) and interaction patterns (Tools/Resources/Responses), makes it an excellent foundation for building complex systems composed of multiple interacting AI agents or specialized microservices, potentially arranged in intricate hierarchies.

- **The Concept:** An MCP component isn't limited to being just a Client or just a Server; it can fulfill both roles. This allows for powerful compositions: a high-level "Orchestrator" AI agent (acting as a Client) might receive a complex user request, decompose it, and delegate sub-tasks by calling Tools on several specialized "Worker" agents (each acting as an MCP Server). These Worker agents might, in turn, need to access data by acting as Clients to a shared "Data Service" (another MCP Server). This creates chains or trees of interaction.
- **MCP's Role:** The protocol provides the essential *lingua franca* and standardized structure for these interactions. Regardless of an agent's position or role in the hierarchy, its communication with adjacent components follows the same predictable patterns of requests, responses, Tool definitions, and Resource access, promoting modularity and interoperability.
- **Complexities to Manage:**
  - **Identity & Permissions:** Securely propagating the original user's identity or task-specific permissions across multiple hops in the hierarchy is non-trivial. Techniques like OAuth token exchange or signed assertions might be needed to ensure each agent acts with the appropriate

authority without needing the user's primary credentials.

- o **Workflow Coordination:** Managing the overall state, handling errors gracefully (what happens if a downstream agent fails?), coordinating parallel tasks, and aggregating results across a distributed workflow requires sophisticated orchestration logic, often residing in the higher-level agents.
- o **Debugging & Observability:** Tracing a single logical request as it flows through multiple agents and identifying performance bottlenecks or points of failure necessitates robust distributed logging (with correlation IDs) and tracing mechanisms (e.g., integrating with standards like OpenTelemetry).

- **Analogy:** Consider a large project delegation within a complex corporation. The CEO (User) sets a strategic objective for a Vice President (Orchestrator Agent). The VP analyzes the objective, breaks it down, and assigns specific tasks (Tool calls) with deadlines to different Department Heads (Worker Agents). A Department Head might need financial data (Resource request) from the central Finance Department (Data Service) and might delegate implementation details (further Tool calls) to their Team Leads. All communication relies on standardized company memos and reporting structures (MCP).

MCP's standardized communication provides the crucial underpinning for building sophisticated, modular, and potentially highly scalable multi-agent AI systems.

Section 5: Handling Interactive Workflows and User Permissions

Many valuable real-world tasks extend beyond a single request-response cycle. They often involve multi-step processes requiring intermediate feedback, clarification, confirmation, or decision-making, frequently involving the end-user directly.

- **Interactive Workflows:** These are multi-turn processes orchestrated typically by the Client application, involving a dynamic interplay between the AI, MCP Tools/Resources, and the user interface. The flow might look like this:
    - AI suggests an action involving a Tool.
    - Client invokes the Tool via MCP Server.
    - Server returns results.
    - Client presents results/options to the user via UI.
    - User provides input/selection/confirmation via UI.
    - Client potentially invokes another Tool based on user input, or confirms/cancels the operation.
    - Sensitive steps might require specific permission checks before execution.
- **MCP's Role:** While the overall orchestration logic usually resides in the Client application, MCP structures the individual communication steps with the Server (ToolRequests, ResourceRequests, Responses) that form part of the workflow. It standardizes how the Client asks the Server to perform actions or retrieve data at each stage.
- **Challenges & Considerations:**
    - **State Management:** The orchestrating component (Client) needs a robust way to maintain the workflow's state across

108

multiple, potentially asynchronous, MCP interactions and user interactions. This might involve state machines, context tokens, or saving intermediate states.

- o **User Interaction Design:** Designing intuitive UI elements to pause the workflow, clearly prompt the user for necessary input or confirmation, and seamlessly resume the process based on their response is critical for a good user experience.
- o **Mid-Workflow Permissions & Security:** A user might initiate a workflow with basic permissions, but a later step might involve a sensitive action (e.g., confirming a large payment, deleting critical data). The MCP Server's Tool implementation *must* re-verify the user's permissions *at the time of executing that sensitive step*, not just rely on initial permissions granted at the start of the workflow. Context might change, or time-based restrictions might apply.

- **Example:** Booking a complex vacation package: AI asks destination/dates -> User replies -> Client calls find_flights Tool -> Server returns flight options -> Client presents options in UI -> User selects a flight -> Client calls find_hotels Tool (passing selected flight details for context) -> Server returns hotel options -> Client presents options -> User selects a hotel -> Client presents final itinerary and total cost, asking for confirmation -> User confirms via UI button -> Client calls book_package Tool (passing all selected details) -> Server performs final permission checks and executes the booking.

MCP provides the standardized communication building blocks, but successfully orchestrating sophisticated interactive workflows requires careful application-level design focusing on state management, UI/UX, and stage-specific security checks.

Section 6: Real-Time Streaming of Results from Long-Running Operations

Waiting potentially minutes for a Tool to complete its work (e.g., running a complex data analysis, processing a large video file, generating a multi-page report) before receiving any feedback can lead to a frustrating user experience and idle applications. **Streaming** provides a mechanism for the Server to send back results incrementally.

- **What it is:** Instead of bundling the entire result into a single ToolResponse sent only upon completion, the MCP Server can send multiple *partial* responses or data chunks *as they become available* during the Tool's execution, over the same MCP connection.
- **Benefits:**
  - **Improved Perceived Responsiveness:** The user or AI sees initial results, progress indicators, or the beginning of the data stream much sooner, making the application feel more interactive and alive.
  - **Parallel Processing:** The Client can start processing, displaying, or analyzing the initial chunks of the result while the Server continues working on generating the subsequent parts.
  - **Handling Large Data:** Allows the transmission of results that might be too large to fit comfortably or efficiently

within memory or a single response message on either the client or server side.

- **Implementation Considerations:**
  - The Server's Tool execution logic needs to be designed specifically to support streaming, yielding partial results periodically rather than buffering everything until the end.
  - The MCP protocol needs a mechanism to handle this. This could involve sending multiple ToolResponse messages linked by a common request ID, potentially with sequence numbers and a flag indicating if a message is partial or the final one. Alternatively, a dedicated streaming message type or protocol extension might be used. A clear termination signal is essential.
  - The MCP Client requires corresponding logic to receive these multiple messages/chunks, potentially reorder them if necessary (using sequence numbers), and progressively assemble, process, or display the complete result stream as it arrives.
- **Analogy:** Streaming is precisely like watching a live video feed or a large movie file online. You start seeing the content almost immediately (initial results), and the video continues to play as more data arrives in chunks over the network. This contrasts sharply with having to download the entire multi-gigabyte video file before you can even start watching the first second (non-streaming).

Streaming significantly enhances the user experience and efficiency for Tools involving long-running computations or large result sets, making applications feel much more dynamic and capable.

These advanced features – Sampling, Roots, Notifications, support for hierarchical systems, interactive workflows, and streaming – showcase the depth, flexibility, and forward-thinking design considerations potentially encompassed by the Model Context Protocol. By understanding and leveraging these capabilities thoughtfully, developers can move beyond basic request-response integrations and build the truly sophisticated, dynamic, context-aware, and responsive AI-powered applications needed to tackle the next generation of complex real-world challenges. Mastering these allows you to push the boundaries of what's possible with AI integration.

CHAPTER 12

Troubleshooting and Best Practices for MCP Development

You've journeyed through the architecture, components, advanced features, and security considerations of the Model Context Protocol. You've designed Servers and Clients, defined Tools and Resources, and explored the power of Prompts and context. Now, it's time to address the practical realities of development: things sometimes go wrong, and efficient practices can save significant time and effort.

Building sophisticated systems involving AI, external services, and standardized communication protocols inevitably presents challenges. This chapter aims to equip you with strategies for troubleshooting common problems encountered during MCP integration and share best practices gleaned from real-world development experiences. Think of this as your field guide for navigating the development terrain smoothly.

We'll cover:

1. **Common Challenges and Pitfalls:** Identifying and understanding frequent hurdles.
2. **Debugging and Testing:** Practical techniques for finding and fixing issues.
3. **Efficient Development & Deployment:** Streamlining your workflow.
4. **Performance Optimization:** Making your MCP applications run smoothly and quickly.

Let's dive into the practical wisdom that helps turn MCP concepts into robust, production-ready applications.

Section 1: Navigating Common Challenges and Pitfalls

Being aware of potential roadblocks can help you anticipate and avoid them. Here are some common issues developers encounter when working with MCP:

- **Definition Mismatches:** The Client's understanding of a Tool or Resource (based on the definition it has) differs from the Server's actual implementation. This could be due to outdated definitions, typos, or misinterpretations of parameter types or output schemas. *Mitigation:* Maintain a single source of truth for definitions (e.g., a shared schema repository), use versioning, and ensure Clients and Servers are using compatible definition versions.
- **Authentication/Authorization Failures:** Problems with obtaining, validating, or handling OAuth tokens are frequent. This might involve incorrect configuration of the Authorization Server, mismatched client IDs/secrets, expired tokens, insufficient token scopes, or errors in the Server's token validation logic. *Mitigation:* Double-check configurations, ensure clock synchronization between systems (important for token expiration checks), use SDKs that handle much of the OAuth complexity correctly, and leverage detailed logging (Chapter 10).
- **State Management Complexity:** Especially in interactive workflows (Chapter 11) or hierarchical agent systems, managing the state of an operation across multiple asynchronous steps and interactions can become very complex and error-prone. *Mitigation:* Use appropriate state management patterns (e.g., state machines), design workflows carefully, ensure correlation IDs are

used consistently, and simplify state requirements where possible.

- **Prompt Engineering Difficulties:** Getting the AI model to reliably understand when to use a specific Tool or Resource, how to format the request correctly, and how to interpret the response often requires significant iteration on prompt design (Chapter 9) and potentially Tool/Resource descriptions. *Mitigation:* Treat prompt engineering as an iterative process. Test prompts extensively, analyze AI failures, refine descriptions and instructions, and consider providing few-shot examples within the prompt.
- **Network Issues:** Simple connectivity problems, firewalls blocking ports (especially for HTTP/SSE), DNS resolution failures, or intermittent network latency can disrupt MCP communication, particularly between remote Clients and Servers. *Mitigation:* Ensure basic network connectivity, check firewall rules, use robust retry mechanisms (especially for idempotent Tools), and implement health checks for Server availability.
- **Asynchronous Complexity:** Correctly handling asynchronous operations like Notifications, streaming responses, or non-blocking Tool execution requires careful programming to avoid race conditions, deadlocks, or missed messages. *Mitigation:* Leverage async/await patterns or callback mechanisms provided by your language/SDK, carefully manage concurrency, and ensure reliable handling of message sequences (e.g., for streaming or notifications).

Analogy: Building with a complex LEGO Technic set requires ensuring the right pieces connect perfectly (definitions), the motor has power and is wired correctly (auth/auth), complex gear trains mesh smoothly (state management), and the remote control signals are clear (prompts). Sometimes connections are physically tricky (network/async).

Section 2: Debugging and Testing MCP Systems

When things go wrong, systematic debugging and thorough testing are essential.

- **Leverage Logging:** As emphasized in Chapter 10, detailed, structured logging on *both* the Client and Server is your most powerful debugging tool. Log requests, responses, parameters (non-sensitive ones!), errors, correlation IDs, timestamps, and key decision points. Use consistent log levels (DEBUG, INFO, WARN, ERROR).
- **Distributed Tracing:** In hierarchical systems (Chapter 11) where a request might pass through multiple MCP components, distributed tracing (using standards like OpenTelemetry and tools like Jaeger or Zipkin) is invaluable. It allows you to visualize the entire lifecycle of a request across services, pinpointing bottlenecks or where an error originated. Ensure correlation IDs are propagated across hops.
- **SDK Debugging Features:** Explore if your chosen MCP SDK offers specific debugging modes, verbose logging options, or utilities for inspecting messages or connection states.
- **Testing Strategies Revisited:**
  - **Unit Tests:** Isolate and test individual components: Tool implementation logic (mocking dependencies), Resource data retrieval logic, prompt generation

functions, message serialization/deserialization logic.

- o **Integration Tests:** Test the interaction between your MCP Client and Server over the chosen transport (stdio or HTTP/SSE). Mock the *external* dependencies of the Server (e.g., databases, third-party APIs called by Tools) but test the actual MCP communication and request/response handling.
- o **End-to-End (E2E) Tests:** Test the entire flow, potentially including the actual AI model interaction. These tests are the most realistic but can be complex, expensive, and non-deterministic (due to AI variability). Use them judiciously for critical user journeys.
- o **Failure Injection / Chaos Testing:** Intentionally simulate failures (e.g., network timeouts, Tool errors, Resource unavailability, invalid responses) to verify that your system handles errors gracefully, retries appropriately, and doesn't cascade failures.
- **Debugging Tools:** Utilize standard development tools:
  - o **Network Sniffers/Inspectors:** Tools like Wireshark (for general network traffic) or browser developer tools (for inspecting SSE connections over HTTPS) can help analyze the raw message exchange.
  - o **API Clients:** Tools like Postman or curl can be useful for manually sending requests to your MCP Server's HTTP endpoints during development and debugging.

Section 3: Strategies for Efficient Development and Deployment

Streamlining your development process helps you build and iterate faster.

- **Maximize SDK Usage:** Fully leverage the features provided by the official MCP SDKs for your language. They handle much of the protocol boilerplate (message formatting, validation, transport management), letting you focus on application logic. Avoid reimplementing core protocol handling unless absolutely necessary.
- **Clear, Versioned Definitions:** Treat your Tool and Resource definitions as critical artifacts. Store them in a version-controlled system (like Git), potentially in a format like JSON Schema or OpenAPI that can be shared and validated. Ensure Clients and Servers agree on definition versions.
- **Modularity:** Design Tools and Resources as self-contained, reusable components where possible. This improves testability and maintainability.
- **Automated Testing (CI/CD):** Integrate your unit and integration tests into Continuous Integration/Continuous Deployment (CI/CD) pipelines. Automatically run tests on every code change to catch regressions early. Automate deployment processes for both Client and Server components.
- **API Versioning:** If you need to make breaking changes to your Tools or Resources, implement an API versioning strategy for your MCP Server (e.g., via URL path, custom headers) to allow older clients to continue functioning while you roll out new versions.
- **Environment Configuration:** Use configuration files or environment variables to manage settings

like Server URLs, API keys, database connection strings, and feature flags across different environments (development, testing, staging, production). Avoid hardcoding these values.

Section 4: Performance Optimization

As your MCP application scales, performance becomes increasingly important.

- **Efficient Resource Design:** Design Resources to return only the data needed for typical use cases. Avoid fetching and transmitting huge amounts of data if only a small subset is required. Consider adding parameters to Resource requests to allow clients to specify filtering or data projection needs.
- **Server-Side Caching:** Implement caching strategies (as discussed in Chapter 9) on the Server for frequently accessed Resource data that doesn't change very often. This reduces load on backend systems and speeds up responses. Choose appropriate cache invalidation strategies.
- **Asynchronous Operations:** For Tools that perform long-running tasks but don't need to block the Client, implement them asynchronously on the Server. The Tool can return an immediate acknowledgment, and the final result or status can be delivered later via a Notification (Chapter 11).
- **Streaming:** For Tools that generate large results incrementally, use streaming (Chapter 11) to send data back to the Client as it becomes available, improving perceived performance and reducing memory pressure.
- **Transport Choice & Overhead:** For local Client-Server interactions on the same machine, the stdio transport generally has lower overhead than HTTP/SSE. For remote interactions, consider the

efficiency of your HTTP server and SSE implementation.

- **Payload Size Optimization:** Be mindful of the size of data being sent in MCP messages (Tool parameters, Resource/Tool results). Use efficient data formats (e.g., prefer concise identifiers over verbose descriptions if the client can look them up), and avoid sending redundant information.
- **Load Testing:** Before deploying to production or anticipating significant load increases, perform load testing against your MCP Server to identify performance bottlenecks. Simulate realistic request patterns and volumes to understand how your server scales and where optimizations might be needed (e.g., database query optimization, scaling server instances).

Building robust applications with the Model Context Protocol, like any software development endeavor, involves encountering challenges, debugging issues, and continuously refining your approach. By anticipating common pitfalls, employing systematic debugging and testing techniques, adopting efficient development workflows, and paying attention to performance, you can navigate the complexities effectively. Remember that development is often an iterative process; embrace learning from issues, refining your designs, and leveraging the best practices shared here to build truly powerful and reliable MCP-enabled AI integrations.

CHAPTER 13

Real-World Applications and Use Cases of MCP

Having explored the technical foundations, advanced features, and best practices of the Model Context Protocol, let's now look at where the rubber meets the road. How is MCP actually being used today, and what exciting possibilities does it unlock for the future? Theory is valuable, but seeing the protocol in action truly highlights its transformative potential.

MCP isn't just an abstract specification; it's a practical solution enabling a new generation of integrated AI experiences. From enhancing developer productivity in IDEs to streamlining complex enterprise workflows and powering innovative desktop applications, MCP provides the common language needed for AI and software components to collaborate effectively.

This chapter will showcase concrete examples and explore potential applications across various domains:

1. **MCP in Action:** Highlighting current implementations in IDEs, desktop apps, enterprise systems, and specific tool integrations.
2. **Exploring the Horizon:** Brainstorming potential use cases across diverse industries.

Prepare to be inspired by the breadth and depth of applications made possible by the Model Context Protocol!

Section 1: MCP in Action: Current Implementations

MCP is already enabling powerful integrations in various software environments. Here are some key examples:

- **Integrated Development Environments (IDEs):** This is a prime area for MCP. AI coding assistants, whether running locally or remotely, can act as MCP Servers or Clients.
  - *Tools:* refactor_code, generate_unit_tests, explain_code_snippet, run_build, debug_step_over.
  - *Resources:* current_file_content, project_symbol_tree, compiler_errors, debugger_state.
  - *Impact:* MCP allows AI assistants to deeply integrate into the coding workflow, understanding the context of the code being written (via Resources) and taking meaningful actions within the IDE (via Tools), significantly boosting developer productivity and capability.
- **Desktop AI Applications:** For AI assistants or models running locally on a user's machine, MCP (often using the stdio transport) provides a standardized way to interact with the operating system or other desktop applications.
  - *Tools:* open_application, create_file, adjust_system_volume, read_clipboard_to_user.
  - *Resources:* get_clipboard_content, list_running_processes, get_active_window_title.
  - *Impact:* Empowers local AI applications to go beyond simple text generation and become helpful agents capable of performing tasks directly on the user's computer in a controlled manner.
- **Enterprise Integrations:** MCP offers a standardized approach for connecting powerful AI

models (potentially hosted centrally or externally) with complex internal enterprise systems, overcoming the challenges of bespoke integrations for each system.

- *Examples:*
  - Connecting an AI to a payment platform like **Block (Square)**: Tool: process_refund, Resource: get_transaction_details.
  - Interfacing with a GraphQL API gateway like **Apollo**: Tool: execute_graphql_mutation, Resource: execute_graphql_query.
- *Impact:* Enables AI to securely access enterprise data (Resources) and trigger business processes (Tools) according to established permissions (often managed via OAuth 2.1, as discussed in Chapter 10), streamlining workflows like customer support, data analysis, and process automation.

- **Specific Tool Integrations:** The flexibility of MCP allows AI to connect to a vast array of specific software tools:
  - **Blender:** Tool: render_scene_frame, apply_modifier; Resource: get_object_properties. Enables AI-driven 3D modeling and rendering tasks.
  - **Notion:** Tool: create_database_entry, append_to_page; Resource: search_workspace, get_page_block_content. Allows AI to act as a knowledge management assistant.
  - **GitHub:** Tool: create_pull_request_comment, assign_issue; Resource: get_file_diff, list_repository_issues. Integrates AI into software development lifecycles.

- Stripe: Tool: create_customer_subscription, cancel_invoice; Resource: get_customer_payment_methods. Enables AI participation in billing and payment workflows.
- Slack: Tool: post_message_to_channel, set_user_status; Resource: get_channel_members, search_messages. Allows AI agents to communicate and collaborate within team environments.
- Databases: Resource: execute_read_only_sql (for fetching data); Tool: execute_parameterized_update (use write-access Tools with extreme caution and strict permissions!). Enables AI to query and potentially modify application data directly.

These examples illustrate how MCP acts as a universal adapter, allowing AI to plug into diverse software ecosystems.

Section 2: Exploring the Horizon: Potential Across Industries

The potential applications of MCP extend far beyond current implementations. Its ability to safely connect AI reasoning with specific data and actions opens doors in nearly every industry:

- **Finance:**
  - AI analyzing real-time market data feeds (Resources) and executing trades based on predefined strategies (Tools).
  - Automated fraud detection systems accessing transaction histories (Resources)

and flagging suspicious activities or initiating blocks (Tools).

- o Personalized financial advisory bots retrieving account information (Resources) and suggesting portfolio adjustments (potentially via Tools requiring user confirmation).
- **Healthcare:** (Requires strict adherence to privacy regulations like HIPAA)
  - o AI diagnostic assistants accessing anonymized patient medical history and imaging reports (Resources) to suggest potential diagnoses or relevant research papers.
  - o Automated appointment scheduling systems checking doctor availability (Resources) and booking slots (Tools).
  - o AI tools summarizing lengthy medical research papers or clinical trial results (Resources/Tools) for busy clinicians.
- **Legal:**
  - o AI contract review tools analyzing legal documents (Resources) to identify specific clauses, potential risks, or deviations from templates.
  - o Automated document drafting assistants using approved templates (Prompts) and case details (Resources) to generate initial drafts of contracts or filings (Tools).
  - o AI-powered legal research assistants querying legal databases (Resources) and summarizing relevant case law.
- **Supply Chain & Logistics:**
  - o AI systems optimizing inventory management by accessing real-time stock levels across warehouses (Resources) and

automatically generating reorder requests (Tools).

- o Predictive maintenance systems analyzing sensor data from vehicles or machinery (Resources) and scheduling maintenance appointments (Tools).
- o Route optimization engines accessing traffic data and delivery schedules (Resources) to plan efficient routes for delivery fleets.

- **Customer Support:**
  - o AI support agents accessing customer order history and knowledge bases (Resources) to provide instant answers or troubleshoot issues.
  - o Automated return/refund processing systems verifying purchase details (Resources) and initiating refund transactions (Tools).
  - o Intelligent escalation systems identifying complex issues beyond the AI's capability and routing them to the appropriate human agent with relevant context (Tools/Resources).

- **Personal Productivity:**
  - o AI assistants managing personal calendars by checking availability (Resources) and scheduling meetings (Tools).
  - o Note-taking apps where AI can summarize meeting transcripts (Resources) and create action items (Tools).
  - o AI automating email sorting, drafting replies based on context (Resources/Prompts/Tools), and managing tasks lists.

- o Integration with smart home devices via MCP, allowing AI to control lights, thermostats, or appliances (Tools/Resources).

These are just glimpses of the possibilities. As AI models become more capable and the MCP ecosystem matures, we can expect to see even more innovative and impactful applications emerge.

From streamlining code development to managing complex enterprise data and potentially revolutionizing entire industries, the Model Context Protocol provides the essential connective tissue for integrating AI intelligence into the fabric of our digital world. Its focus on standardization, security, and clear definitions for capabilities paves the way for a future where AI doesn't just reside in isolated models but actively and safely collaborates with the software and systems we use every day. The journey of MCP is just beginning, and its potential impact is truly exciting.

CHAPTER 14

The Growing MCP Ecosystem and Community

Throughout this book, we've explored the technical intricacies and powerful potential of the Model Context Protocol. But MCP is more than just a specification; it's the foundation for a growing ecosystem and the focal point for a vibrant community of developers, researchers, and innovators passionate about the future of AI integration. A protocol's true strength often lies in the community that adopts, extends, and supports it.

As you embark on your journey with MCP, understanding this ecosystem and knowing how to engage with the community is invaluable. Whether you're looking for existing integrations, seeking help with a challenge, or wanting to contribute back, the MCP community is your greatest resource.

This chapter shines a light on the human element and shared infrastructure surrounding MCP:

1. **The Vibrant Community:** Exploring the developers and contributors driving MCP forward.
2. **Discovering Integrations:** Navigating server registries to find existing MCP capabilities.
3. **Contributing Back:** How you can help shape the future of the MCP open standard.
4. **Key Players:** Recognizing the role of organizations like Anthropic and others in the ecosystem.

Let's explore the ecosystem and invite you to join this exciting endeavor!

Section 1: The Heartbeat: The MCP Developer Community

MCP development doesn't happen in isolation. It's fueled by an active, collaborative, and expanding community of individuals and organizations working together. This community is where ideas are exchanged, problems are solved, and the protocol evolves.

- **Where to Connect:** You can typically find the MCP community congregating on various platforms (as mentioned in Chapter 5):
    - **Official Forums/Mailing Lists:** For structured discussions, proposals, and announcements.
    - **Real-Time Chat (Discord/Slack):** For quick questions, informal discussions, and real-time collaboration.
    - **Code Repositories (GitHub etc.):** For accessing the specification source, SDKs, reporting issues, and contributing code or documentation.
- **Benefits of Participation:** Engaging with the community offers numerous advantages:
    - **Get Help:** Stuck on an implementation detail? Chances are someone else has faced a similar issue and can offer guidance.
    - **Share Knowledge:** Share your successes, solutions, and best practices to help others.
    - **Find Collaborators:** Connect with others working on similar projects or integrations.
    - **Stay Updated:** Be the first to know about new developments, SDK releases, and proposed changes to the standard.
    - **Influence Direction:** Participate in discussions that shape the future evolution of MCP.

- **Analogy:** Think of the MCP community as a bustling, collaborative workshop or town square. People gather to share blueprints (ideas), lend tools (code snippets), help troubleshoot tricky constructions (debugging), and collectively build amazing things (MCP applications).

Whether you're a seasoned developer or just starting, your participation is welcome and valuable.

Section 2: Discovering Integrations: Server Registries

As more developers build MCP Servers exposing Tools and Resources for various applications (like Notion, GitHub, Blender, etc., mentioned in Chapter 13), how do you find them? This is where the concept of **MCP Server Registries** comes in.

- **What They Are (Conceptually):** Imagine centralized directories or marketplaces where developers can list their publicly available MCP Servers. These registries would act as discovery mechanisms for MCP Clients.
- **How They Might Work:** A registry could allow searching or browsing based on the application integrated (e.g., "Slack", "Stripe"), the capabilities offered (specific Tool/Resource names), or keywords. Listings might include:
  - Server Name and Description
  - Connection Endpoint URL (for SSE transport)
  - Authentication requirements (e.g., OAuth 2.1 scopes needed)
  - List of available Tools and Resources (potentially linking to their definitions)

- o Maintainer information and documentation links.
- **Benefits:**
  - o **Simplified Discovery:** Makes it much easier for developers to find and integrate existing MCP capabilities without building everything from scratch.
  - o **Promotes Reuse:** Encourages sharing and standardization, reducing duplicated effort across the ecosystem.
  - o **Fosters Growth:** A thriving registry signals a healthy and active ecosystem, attracting more developers and users.
- **Considerations:** The success of registries depends on community adoption, mechanisms for keeping listings up-to-date, and potentially processes for verifying the quality or security posture of listed servers.

Keep an eye out for emerging MCP server registries as the ecosystem matures – they will be key hubs for finding pre-built integrations.

Section 3: Shaping the Future: Contributing to MCP

MCP is often developed as an open standard, meaning its evolution is driven by community collaboration. You have the opportunity to contribute directly to its future!

- **Ways to Contribute:**
  - o **To the Standard Itself:** Engage in discussions on the official forums or mailing lists. If you have ideas for improvements, new features, or clarifications, follow the defined contribution process (often involving

opening issues or pull requests on the specification's repository) to propose changes.

- o **To SDKs:** Help improve the official Software Development Kits. This can involve reporting bugs you find, submitting fixes (pull requests), enhancing the documentation, adding more examples, or even developing an SDK for a currently unsupported language.
- o **To Tooling & Infrastructure:** Develop helper libraries, validation tools, debugging utilities, testing frameworks, reference implementations, or even help build and maintain server registries.
- o **Create and Share Integrations:** Build MCP Servers for popular applications, services, or APIs that don't have one yet. Share your work (perhaps listing it in a registry) for others to use. Create example client applications demonstrating best practices.
- **Everyone Can Help:** Contributions aren't limited to writing code. Improving documentation, participating in discussions, helping answer questions from other users, and providing thoughtful feedback are all incredibly valuable ways to contribute to the health and growth of the MCP ecosystem.

Your involvement, no matter the scale, helps make MCP better for everyone.

Section 4: Key Players and Ecosystem Growth

While MCP thrives on broad community participation, the involvement of key organizations often plays a significant role in driving initial development, standardization, and adoption.

- **Anthropic's Role:** Organizations like Anthropic have been instrumental in pioneering and promoting concepts closely related to or directly involving MCP, particularly in the context of enabling large language models to interact safely and effectively with external tools. Their research, development, and advocacy lend significant weight and direction to the ecosystem.
- **Other Major Players:** As MCP gains traction, expect to see wider adoption and support from other major AI labs, cloud providers, enterprise software companies, and open-source foundations. Their involvement can manifest as:
  - Native support for MCP in their AI models or platforms.
  - Development of official SDKs and tooling.
  - Creation of MCP integrations for their own products and services.
  - Participation in standardization efforts.
- **A Collaborative Ecosystem:** While key players provide momentum, the goal of an open standard like MCP is to foster a diverse and collaborative ecosystem where contributions from individuals, startups, academic institutions, and large corporations are all valued. The interplay between these different actors drives innovation and ensures the protocol meets a wide range of needs.

The growing support from various players signifies confidence in MCP's approach and points towards a future where it becomes a ubiquitous standard for AI integration.

The Model Context Protocol is more than just technical specifications; it's a shared vision for seamless, secure, and powerful AI integration, brought to life by a dynamic and growing global community. By understanding the ecosystem, leveraging available resources, engaging with fellow developers, and perhaps even contributing back yourself, you become an active participant in shaping this exciting future. We encourage you to connect with the community, explore existing integrations, and consider how you can contribute to the ongoing journey of MCP. Welcome aboard!

CHAPTER 15

The Future of MCP: Roadmap and Potential Developments

Throughout this book, we've journeyed from the fundamental concepts of the Model Context Protocol to its advanced features, applications, and community ecosystem. But the story of MCP is far from over; it's a living, evolving standard with a dynamic future. As AI capabilities continue to advance and integration needs become more sophisticated, MCP is poised to adapt and grow.

Understanding the potential future direction of MCP can help you anticipate upcoming features, align your development efforts, and even contribute to shaping its evolution. This chapter offers a glimpse into the anticipated roadmap and potential developments, based on current trends, community discussions, and logical next steps.

Let's explore what the future might hold for MCP:

1. **Near-Term Priorities (2025 Focus):** Key areas of development expected in the near future.
2. **Standardizing Remote Interactions:** Enhancing security and discovery for networked MCP.
3. **Modern Architectures:** Supporting stateless operations and serverless environments.
4. **Expanding Horizons:** Moving beyond text to other modalities like audio and video.
5. **Formal Standardization:** The path towards broader industry adoption and recognition.

Join us as we look ahead to the continuing evolution of AI integration.

Section 1: The Road Ahead: Near-Term Priorities (2025 Focus)

While roadmaps evolve, several key areas appear poised for significant focus in the near future (looking towards the 2025 timeframe and beyond) to enhance MCP's usability and power:

- **Robust Remote Support:** While remote communication via HTTP/SSE exists, expect continued efforts to make these interactions more seamless, performant, and feature-rich. This includes refining the protocol for efficiency, potentially embracing Streamable HTTP (as mentioned in Chapter 4), and standardizing common patterns for remote use cases.
- **Enhanced Agent Capabilities:** As AI agents become more autonomous and capable of handling complex, multi-step tasks, MCP will likely evolve to better support them. This could involve richer ways to define Tool capabilities (e.g., specifying dependencies, pre/post-conditions), improved mechanisms for state management across interactions, better support for coordinating hierarchical agent systems (Chapter 11), and perhaps more sophisticated ways for agents to discover and select appropriate tools dynamically.
- **Developer Resources & Tooling:** Lowering the barrier to entry and improving the developer experience is crucial for adoption. Expect continued investment in:
  - **SDKs:** Expanding language support, adding features, improving performance, and enhancing documentation.
  - **Documentation:** More tutorials, best practice guides, detailed examples, and clearer specification explanations.

- o **Testing Tools:** Frameworks and utilities specifically designed for testing MCP Clients and Servers.
- o **Reference Implementations:** Providing well-maintained examples to guide developers.

These priorities focus on making MCP more powerful, easier to use, and more applicable to complex, real-world scenarios, particularly those involving networked communication and sophisticated AI agents.

Section 2: Standardizing Remote Interactions

As remote MCP usage grows, standardizing common patterns for security and discovery becomes increasingly important for interoperability and ease of use.

- **Standardized Authentication & Authorization:** While OAuth 2.1 (Chapter 10) provides a strong foundation, the MCP community might define specific profiles or best practice recommendations for using OAuth 2.1/OpenID Connect within the MCP context. This could involve standardizing token formats, scope definitions relevant to MCP operations (e.g., mcp:tool:execute:send_email, mcp:resource:read:user_profile), and secure patterns for token validation and exchange, ensuring different MCP implementations can securely interoperate.
- **Standardized Service Discovery:** The concept of Server Registries (Chapter 14) could evolve into a more formalized discovery mechanism. This might involve defining a standard protocol for:

- Clients to query a registry for servers offering specific capabilities.
- Clients to directly query an MCP Server endpoint (perhaps a well-known URI) to retrieve its capabilities manifest (list of Tools/Resources).
  Standardizing discovery would make it much easier for clients to dynamically find and connect to relevant MCP services in a distributed environment.

These efforts aim to make networked MCP interactions as seamless and secure as local ones.

Section 3: Embracing Modern Architectures: Statelessness and Serverless

Modern software development increasingly favors stateless services and serverless computing models (like AWS Lambda, Google Cloud Functions, Azure Functions) for scalability and cost-efficiency. MCP may evolve to better align with these paradigms.

- **Stateless Operations:** While some MCP interactions inherently involve state (like long-running tools or interactive workflows), future protocol versions or profiles might emphasize patterns that minimize server-side state-holding. This could involve ensuring requests contain all necessary context or using mechanisms like signed state tokens passed back and forth between client and server.
- **Serverless Environments:** Adapting MCP transports and interaction patterns for serverless functions presents unique challenges (e.g., managing persistent SSE connections). Future

developments might include specific guidance, SDK adaptations, or even alternative transport mechanisms (perhaps based on message queues or webhooks) better suited for ephemeral, event-driven serverless architectures.

Supporting these architectures would broaden MCP's applicability to cloud-native application development.

Section 4: Expanding Horizons: Beyond Text

Much of the current focus in AI integration revolves around text-based interactions. However, AI is rapidly expanding into other modalities, and MCP has the potential to evolve alongside it.

- **Potential New Modalities:** Future versions of MCP could introduce standardized ways to handle:
    - **Audio:** Defining Tools for operations like real-time transcription, text-to-speech synthesis, speaker identification, or audio analysis. Resources could represent audio streams or files.
    - **Video:** Tools for video summarization, object detection within frames, activity recognition, or video generation. Resources could provide video feeds or file access.
    - **Images:** Tools for image generation (text-to-image), image editing/manipulation, or image analysis (object recognition, OCR). Resources could represent image files or pixel data.
    - **Structured Data:** Beyond simple JSON, perhaps richer support for interacting with

specific structured data formats or databases.

- **Challenges:** Standardizing interactions across diverse modalities presents significant challenges, requiring careful consideration of data formats, streaming protocols, and capability definitions. However, extending MCP could provide a unified framework for AI to interact with a much wider range of digital information and tools.

Expanding beyond text would position MCP as a truly comprehensive protocol for general-purpose AI interaction with the digital world.

Section 5: Towards Formal Standardization and Broader Adoption

For MCP to achieve widespread, long-term success and interoperability, moving towards formal standardization could be a key step.

- **The Path:** This might involve submitting the MCP specification to established standards bodies like the Internet Engineering Task Force (IETF) or the World Wide Web Consortium (W3C), or potentially forming a dedicated foundation or consortium focused on its development and governance (similar to initiatives like OpenAPI or GraphQL).
- **Benefits of Formalization:**
  - **Increased Trust & Stability:** Formal standards signal maturity and long-term commitment, encouraging broader industry adoption.
  - **Guaranteed Interoperability:** Rigorous standardization processes help ensure that

different implementations can reliably work together.

- o **Clear Governance:** Establishes clear processes for evolving the standard, managing contributions, and resolving ambiguities.
- o **Wider Recognition:** Increases visibility and credibility within the broader software engineering community.
- **Community Role:** The drive towards formal standardization often requires significant effort and consensus-building within the existing community and key industry players (as discussed in Chapter 14).

Formal standardization could solidify MCP's position as a fundamental building block for the future of integrated AI.

The future of the Model Context Protocol is bright and full of potential. Driven by the needs of increasingly sophisticated AI applications and guided by a collaborative community, MCP is set to evolve, becoming more robust, versatile, and easier to use. From enhancing remote communication and supporting modern architectures to potentially embracing new modalities and achieving formal standardization, the journey ahead promises exciting developments. By understanding this roadmap, you are not just prepared to use MCP today, but also positioned to participate in and benefit from its evolution tomorrow. The future of AI integration is being built now, and MCP is a key part of that foundation.

www.ingramcontent.com/pod-product-compliance
Lightning Source LLC
LaVergne TN
LVHW051653050326
832903LV00032B/3789